Law of Three: Catalyst of Existence

by

Nora Igwe

Preface

Every story of creation, every unfolding of life, every moment of becoming, begins with a spark. In science, we call it a catalyst, a force that quickens change without being diminished. In philosophy, it is known as the hidden pulse beneath the fabric of existence. Across cultures, it appears as a pattern: The power of three. From the mind's architecture of id, ego, and superego, to the eternal balance of birth, life, and death, the triad is both blueprint and breath of reality.

The Lawof Three: Catalyst of Existence is an exploration of this universal rhythm, the silent principle that shapes thought, guides evolution, and weaves harmony between opposing forces. It is the unseen hand that turns potential into form, and form into transformation. To understand it is to glimpse the code of creation itself.

Table of Contents

Introduction 4

Part I 7

The Pattern Beneath All Things 7

Chapter 1 8

The Law of Three: Catalysts of Existence 8

Chapter 2 27

The Catalyst Principle 27

Chapter 3 40

The Cosmic Triad 40

Part II 56

The Triad Within: Mind and Self 56

Chapter 4 58

Freud's Threefold Mind 58

Chapter 5 77

The Inner Dance of Three 77

Chapter 6 93

Shadow, Light, and Integration 93

Part III 113

The Law of Three in the World 113

Chapter 7 115

Three in Relationships 115

Chapter 8 130

Three in Society and History 130

Chapter 9 143

The Hidden Third 143

Part IV 154

Living the Catalyst 154

Chapter 10 155

Working with the Law of Three 155

Chapter 11 164

The Power of Conscious Triads 164

Chapter 12 173

The Endless Spiral 173

Closing Reflections 180

The Catalyst of Existence 180

Conclusion 182

Embracing the Catalyst 182

Introduction

From the spiral of galaxies to the quiet rhythm of our breath, life moves in patterns. We often notice the obvious cycles day and night, growth and decay, joy and sorrow, but beneath these visible motions lies a subtler architecture. The Law of Three is one such design. It is not just a number; it is a principle woven into the very DNA of existence.

The ancients knew it as a sacred rhythm: The threefold paths of the soul, the triple forces of creation, preservation, and transformation.

Philosophers have called it the foundation of logic: thesis, antithesis, and synthesis. Psychologists see it mirrored in the mind's structure: the id, the ego, and the superego. Even nature hums this triadic tune: seed, growth, bloom; liquid, solid, gas; past, present, future.

A catalyst is an agent that initiates change, accelerates transformation, or reveals potential without being consumed. The Law of Three acts as such a force, quietly shaping order out of chaos and harmony out of tension. It operates in the seen and the unseen, influencing the way we think, love, create, and evolve.

This book is not an attempt to claim ownership of the idea of three; the three is older than any culture, older than the written word, older than me and you. Instead, it is an invitation to explore how this universal pattern reveals itself across mind, matter, and spirit. We will walk through the corridors of psychology, understanding how the id's primal drives, the ego's reason, and the superego's moral compass are not competing enemies but essential pillars of the self. We will travel through the landscapes of philosophy and science, tracing the triads that shape both thought and nature. And we will pause in the quiet space between, where mystery dwells, to consider how the Law of Three can guide us toward balance and clarity in a world that often feels divided.

To see the Law of Three is to recognize that creation is not random. There is a symmetry in the way life unfolds, a deliberate tension that births harmony. And when we learn to work with this principle, to hold its forces in our awareness, we begin to move with the current of existence, rather than against it.

The journey ahead is both intellectual and personal. It will challenge how you see yourself, how you interpret the world, and how you understand the relationships between opposites. For in the dance of three, every conflict has the seed of resolution, every division holds the potential for unity, and every beginning already whispers its end.

Welcome to the Catalyst of Existence.

Part I

The Pattern Beneath All Things

Chapter 1

The Law of Three: Catalysts of Existence

In the beginning, there was only the One, boundless, silent, infinite. From its stillness arose a yearning, a desire to become, to know itself beyond itself. And so, it breathed, and from that breath came the Two, a reflection, a mirror of what was, a tension of opposites. Light and shadow. Motion and stillness. Life and death.

For a time, the One and the Two existed, but nothing stirred. The One alone could not move, and the Two, in its endless polarity, could not create. Thus came the Third, a spark, a bridge, a secret whispered into the cosmos. Where there had been silence, now there was music. Where there had been opposition, now there was flow. The Three danced, and from their rhythm, the worlds were born.

This sacred triad is the catalyst of existence. It does not destroy what came before, nor does it simply add to it. It transforms. It turns potential into reality. Stillness into motion. Tension into creation.

The Triangle of Existence

The triangle, the simplest, strongest of shapes, carries the same truth. Its strength does not lie in one side or two points, but in the dynamic balance of three. In every corner of life, this pattern appears:

- **In Nature**: Seed, soil, and sun awaken life.
- **In Human Experience**: Body, mind, and spirit intertwine.
- **In Time**: Past, present, and future keep the wheel of becoming turning.

Everywhere, three points converge to create stability, movement, and transformation.

The Mystical Completeness of Three

Three completes what one cannot and balances what two cannot reconcile. The ancients recognized it intuitively:

- **The Christian Trinity**: Father, Son, Holy Spirit.
- **The Hindu Trimurti**: Brahma, Vishnu, Shiva.
- **The Celtic Triple Goddess**: Maiden, Mother, Crone.

- **The Greek Moirai**: Spinning, measuring, and cutting the thread of life.

In each culture, the third is always the catalyst; the spark that turns polarity into creation. Tension into flow. Thought into life.

To live by the Law of Three is to see the hidden bridge in every moment:

- In conflict, seek the third path that reconciles opposites.
- In dreams, balance imagination and discipline, letting inspiration ignite the journey.
- In silence, honor the voice, the listener, and the sacred space where understanding arises.

The pattern beneath all things is not chaos, but a living rhythm. The One, Two, and always, the Third, move together to awaken life.

Three is the eternal catalyst, the hidden pulse of existence, the mystical pattern beneath all things.

The Symbolic and Archetypal Nature of Three

The number three is more than mathematics; it is a universal symbol that recurs across myths, religions, psychology, and even the natural

world. It represents wholeness, balance, and transformation; the point at which duality becomes dynamic, and creation emerges.

Three as Wholeness

- **Unity in Multiplicity**: One is unity; two is polarity; three is synthesis. The third completes what the first two cannot.

Examples:

  - The beginning, middle, and end of every story.
  - The past, present, and future of time.
  - Body, mind, and spirit in human experience.

Three represents the whole of existence in motion; not static, not divided, but integrated.

1. Three as Transformation

- The third element in any system acts as a catalyst. It turns tension into movement. Possibility into reality.

Examples:

  - **Alchemical Triads**: Sulfur, mercury, and salt, the spiritual, mental, and physical components of transformation.
  - **In Psychology**: The id, ego, and superego create the dynamic of consciousness.

Without the third, creation stalls. With the third, life evolves.

2. Three as Divine or Sacred

Across cultures, three carries a sacred or mystical resonance:

- **Christianity**: Father, Son, Holy Spirit.
- **Hinduism**: Brahma (creator), Vishnu (preserver), Shiva (destroyer).
- **Celtic Myth**: Maiden, Mother, Crone.

- **Greek Mythology**: The Moirai, spinning, measuring, cutting the thread of life.

The third is often the bridge between the Divine and human; the unseen force that makes the sacred present in the mundane.

3. Three in Nature

- **Physical Systems**: Atoms consist of protons, neutrons, and electrons.

- **Celestial Bodies**: Many cosmologies describe triads in stars, planets, and cosmic cycles.

- **Natural Rhythms**: Dawn, noon, and dusk; birth, life, and death; seed, soil, and sun.

Nature itself mirrors the archetype of three, reinforcing that it is not merely symbolic; it is structural.

Three in Human Consciousness

- Triads appear instinctively in human thought:

  - **Logic and Storytelling**: Problem, reaction, solution, or set-up, confrontation, resolution.

- **Emotion and Choice**: Desire, conflict, transformation.
- **Social Structure**: Self, other, and the bond between.

Three resonates deeply because it reflects the pattern of human cognition and perception, a tension that resolves into insight.

The Archetypal Power

The number three carries archetypal weight because it is complete, dynamic, and generative. It embodies:

- Stability and movement (the triangle as the strongest shape).
- Tension and resolution (dualities reconciled by the third).
- Creation and transformation (catalyst principle).

Recognizing three as an archetype is to see life not as isolated events, but as a patterned dance; a rhythm of forces that continually catalyze growth, consciousness, and transformation.

In essence, the number three is both symbolic and archetypal. It is the hidden code of existence, the silent architect beneath life, and the eternal spark that turns duality into creation.

Walking in the Pattern

To live by the Law of Three is to see the hidden bridge in every moment:

- In conflict, seek the third path that reconciles opposites.
- In dreams, balance imagination and discipline, letting inspiration ignite the journey.
- In silence, honor the voice, the listener, and the quiet place where understanding emerges.

The pattern beneath all things is not chaos, but a living rhythm. The One, Two, and always, the Third, move together to awaken life, consciousness, and transformation.

Three is the eternal catalyst, the archetypal spark, the hidden pulse beneath all things. Wherever you look, within or beyond, the Law of Three unfolds, turning stillness into motion. Tension into creation. Duality into wholeness.

How Triads Appear in Myth, Religion, Science, and Nature.

A Tale of Three Forces

Long ago, before the stars had settled in the sky, there was only the One, a vast, silent ocean of potential. From its depths arose the Two, a pair of twin forces; Light and Shadow, rising to mirror each other across the void.

Alone, they clashed, creating sparks, but no life emerged.

Then, in a whisper, the Third arrived, a gentle Breath that neither opposed Light nor Shadow, but moved between them. Where the Two had argued, the Third balanced, and where conflict had stilled, the Third breathed life.

Triads Across Domains

The number three appears everywhere, hidden yet undeniable. Across cultures, science, and the natural world, triads serve as catalysts of existence, balancing forces and creating patterns that shape life.

1.Myth

Triads in mythology often represent creation, transformation, and the forces of life:

- **Greek Mythology:** The Moirai (Fates), Clotho (spins the thread of life), Lachesis (measures it), and Atropos (cuts it) symbolize the stages of existence.
- **Egyptian Mythology:** Osiris, Isis, and Horus, the cycle of death, preservation, and rebirth.
- **Norse Mythology**: Odin, Vili, and Vé, who together created the world from chaos.

Symbolic role: Triads often unify contrasting forces, representing harmony, balance, and completeness in myths.

2.Religion

Triads in religion express divine completeness and spiritual order:

- **Christianity:** Father, Son, Holy Spirit; the Trinity embodies unity, relationship, and dynamic divinity.

- **Hinduism**: Brahma (creator), Vishnu (preserver), Shiva (destroyer), the Trimurti represents the cosmic cycle.

- **Celtic Tradition:** Maiden, Mother, Crone, reflecting life stages, wisdom, and transformation.

- **Buddhism:** Buddha, Dharma, Sangha, symbolizing the enlightened path, truth, and community.

Symbolic Role: The third often acts as a unifier or bridge, bringing meaning to dualities.

3.Science

Triads are fundamental in understanding physical, biological, and cognitive systems:

- **Physics**: Atoms are composed of protons, neutrons, and electrons; all three are necessary to form matter.

- **Chemistry**: Sulfur, mercury, and salt in alchemy represent mind, spirit, and body; the triad of transformation.

- **Astronomy**: Sun, Earth, and Moon create cycles of day, night, and tides, shaping life rhythms.

- **Neuroscience**: Brain triads, cognition, emotion, and action, work together for decision-making and consciousness.

Symbolic Role: The triad ensures stability, interaction, and catalytic transformation.

4.Nature

Nature consistently reflects triadic patterns, showing that the Law of Three is structural as well as symbolic:

- **Life Cycle**: Birth, life, and death.

- **Elements**: Seed, soil, sun; all essential for growth.

- **Time of Day**: Dawn, noon, dusk; the rhythm of existence.

- **Ecology**: Predator, prey, and environment; creating balance in ecosystems.

Symbolic Role: Triads in nature maintain balance, continuity, and evolution.

5.Human Experience

- **Psychology**: Id, ego, superego, creating mental balance.

- **Storytelling**: Beginning, middle, end; problem, conflict, resolution.

- **Social Interaction**: Self, other, and the relationship connecting them.

Symbolic Role: Triads serve as frameworks for perception, learning, and growth.

Across all domains, myth, religion, science, and nature, triads are patterns of completeness and catalysts for transformation. They balance opposing forces, create structure, and spark emergence. Recognizing triads is like seeing the invisible threads beneath all things, revealing a universal order that repeats at every scale.

Why *"Three"* Feels Complete to the Human Mind

The number three resonates deeply in human perception, thought, and culture. It carries a sense of wholeness, resolution, and balance, unlike one, which feels solitary, or two, which feels incomplete or tension-filled. There are several reasons for this:

1.Psychological Perception

- The human mind is wired to recognize patterns. One point suggests unity, two points suggest polarity, but three points create structure and closure.

- In cognition and memory, triads are easier to grasp and recall. This is why we often remember lists, stories, and ideas in threes:

  - *"Life, liberty, and the pursuit of happiness."*
  - *"Stop, look, and listen."*
  - *"Beginning, middle, and end."*

Three provides completeness. It introduces a middle or connecting element that resolves tension and creates a sense of wholeness.

2.Conflict and Resolution

- One is static. Two is oppositional. However, Three introduces a synthesizing force, a bridge between extremes.

- Psychologically, the mind craves resolution. The third element allows dualities to reconcile:
    - *"Light, dark, and twilight."*
    - *"Mind, heart, and body."*
    - *"Problem, reaction, solution."*

This synthesis satisfies our innate desire for balance and progression, giving the feeling that the sequence is now *"complete."*

3.Storytelling and Narrative Structure

- Across cultures, narratives often follow triadic structures. The human mind expects three movements because it mirrors the process of understanding:

1. Introduction of Tension or Conflict
2. Complication or Opposition
3. Resolution or Transformation

Three creates rhythm and closure, which is why stories, jokes, and speeches often use three elements.

4.Archetypal and Symbolic Resonance

- Triads appear in religion, myth, and symbolism because humans intuitively sense their completeness:
  - Father, Son, Holy Spirit (Christianity)
  - Brahma, Vishnu, Shiva (Hinduism)
  - Maiden, Mother, Crone (Celtic)
  - The third is not just another number; it is the element that reconciles, transforms, and catalyzes, creating psychological satisfaction and a sense of cosmic order.

5.Neurological Pattern Recognition

Studies in cognitive science show that the human brain prefers odd-numbered groupings, especially three, because it provides both balance and dynamism. Two can feel rigid or incomplete; four can feel excessive. But three strikes a harmonious midpoint, one that is stable, yet dynamic.

The Essence

The human mind senses three as complete because it reflects the pattern of life itself: unity, duality, and synthesis; tension and resolution; beginning, middle, and end. Three is the minimal number that introduces movement, balance, and closure, making it feel inherently satisfying, intuitive, and even sacred.

In essence, three resonates with the human mind because it mirrors the rhythm of existence, where opposites meet, a third force emerges, and creation unfolds. It is the number of wholeness, of synthesis, and of life itself.

Now, as we step back from the story of the One, Two, and Third, we begin to see the pattern beneath all things; a rhythm that shapes the cosmos, the earth, and the human soul. The Third is always present, quietly bridging opposites, catalyzing change, and giving rise to creation.

The Law of Three is not just a principle to study; it is a way to live. It invites us to notice the hidden connections, to seek balance amidst conflict, and to embrace the creative tension that brings transformation.

Where dualities clash, the Third emerges.

Where potential remains dormant, the Third sparks movement.
Where life feels fractured, the Third unites.

In every triad, be it myth, religion, science, nature, or human experience, Three carries a sacred truth: Completion arises not from singularity or duality, but from the dynamic interplay of forces that catalyze life itself.

So, as you move forward, remember the rhythm of three:

- One, the origin
- Two, the tension
- Three, the creation

Observe it in your thoughts, your actions, your relationships, and the world around you. Let the Third be your guide, your spark, your bridge. In doing so, you align with the eternal pulse of existence, the hidden pattern beneath all things, and step consciously into the dance of life.

The One, the Two, and the Third are always present. The question is: Will you recognize the Third and allow it to transform your world?

In the next chapter, we will explore how these triads manifest in everyday life, from our relationships and decisions to our creative work and inner growth. We will see how recognizing and aligning with the Third can transform tension into insight, conflict into harmony, and potential into reality. The dance of three is always with us. Now, it is time to learn how to step into it consciously.

Chapter 2

The Catalyst Principle

If the Law of Three shows us the hidden pattern beneath all things, the Catalyst Principle reveals how to step into that pattern consciously. The Third, the element that bridges duality, resolves tension, and sparks creation, is not just a cosmic force; it is a principle we can activate in our own lives.

Every change, every breakthrough, every transformation begins with a catalyst. Just as a spark ignites a flame, the Third catalyzes movement, turning potential into reality. In relationships, it may be empathy or understanding. In thought, it may be insight or perspective. In creativity, it may be inspiration itself.

The key is to recognize that the catalyst is rarely the first or the second force. It often appears quietly, in the space between opposites; in the moment when tension reaches its peak. It is the hidden agent of transformation, the third presence that moves us from inertia to action, from conflict to resolution, from possibility to creation.

Catalysts in Everyday Life

1. Relationships

Consider a disagreement between two people. Alone, each perspective may feel

rigid and immovable. However, with the introduction of a third element, a pause, a new perspective, or even shared humor, the dynamic shifts, allowing understanding to emerge. Thus, the Third transforms conflict into dialogue; tension into connection.

1. Creativity

Artists, writers, and innovators experience the Third as inspiration. An idea

(first force) and effort (second force) may exist. Yet, creation only emerges when a spark awakens from within or an intuition intervenes. That catalytic moment turns potential into something tangible, memorable, and meaningful.

2. Decision-Making

Life often presents binary choices, leaving us feeling stuck between two paths. A third option, sometimes subtle, unexpected, or counterintuitive, can shift the trajectory, resolving indecision and revealing new possibilities.

3. Personal Growth

Inner tension, between who we are and who we wish to become, is a fertile ground for catalysts. A third force can be mindfulness, self-reflection, or guidance from a mentor. This force transforms struggle into learning, confusion into clarity, and potential into action.

The Science and Psychology of Catalysts

Catalysts operate not only spiritually or symbolically, but also scientifically and psychologically:

a) In chemistry, a catalyst accelerates a reaction without being consumed, enabling transformation with minimal input.

b) In neuroscience, insight often arises in the *"incubation period,"* when the brain unconsciously processes conflicting information before a sudden moment of clarity, the Third force emerging between opposing thoughts.

c) In psychology, cognitive reframing, empathy, or even humor often acts as a third element that resolves interpersonal tension or internal conflict.

Across domains, the principle remains the same: The Third activates change where duality alone cannot.

Defining Catalyst

1. Scientific Definition

In science, particularly chemistry, a catalyst is a substance that accelerates a chemical reaction without being consumed or permanently changed. It does not create the reaction itself, but enables it to occur more efficiently.

Key aspects:

- **Facilitator**: A catalyst enables transformation that might otherwise be slow, impossible, or require more energy.

- **Non-consumptive**: The catalyst is not used up; it can continue to spark multiple reactions.

- **Example**: Enzymes in the human body accelerate biological reactions. Without them, processes like digestion would occur too slowly to sustain life.

Scientific insight: The catalyst is the hidden force that transforms potential into actual change without being part of the reaction's *"visible"* products.

1. Philosophical Definition

Philosophically, a catalyst can be understood as any agent that provokes transformation or change without being itself diminished or destroyed. It exists in the space between forces or ideas, bridging opposites and allowing something new to emerge.

Key aspects:

- **Bridge**: The catalyst mediates between polarities, tensions, or conflicting forces.
- **Transformation**: It is not a passive observer; it is the spark that initiates change.
- **Continuity**: Like its scientific counterpart, it is not consumed; it continues to catalyze other processes.

Example in thought and life:

- A moment of insight during meditation can act as a catalyst, transforming anxiety into clarity.

- A third perspective in a conflict can reconcile opposing positions, allowing growth and understanding to emerge.

Philosophical insight: The catalyst represents the principle of emergence; the hidden agent through which duality transforms into unity, potential becomes reality, and tension becomes creation.

Synthesis: Scientific and Philosophical Catalyst

- In science, the catalyst enables physical transformation.
- In philosophy, the catalyst enables experiential, relational, or cognitive transformation.
- In both, it is the unseen spark that triggers change, operating without losing its own essence.

The catalyst is the Third in action, quiet yet powerful, hidden yet transformative, bridging *"what is"* with *"what could be."*

How Catalysts Transform Without Being Consumed

1. Scientific Perspective

In chemistry, a catalyst accelerates a reaction without itself undergoing permanent change. Its essence is to facilitate transformation, not to become part of the outcome.

- **Mechanism**: A catalyst provides an alternate pathway for the reaction with lower energy, allowing molecules to interact more efficiently.

- **Non-consumptive Nature:** After the reaction occurs, the catalyst remains unchanged, ready to catalyze subsequent reactions.

- **Example**: Enzymes in the body speed up digestion. The enzyme is not altered or used up; it can continue catalyzing thousands of reactions.

Insight: Catalyst is the hidden force enabling change, and not the by-product of change. Its role is to bridge potential into actualization without depletion.

2.Philosophical Perspective

Philosophically, a catalyst mediates tension or duality without losing its essence. It is the spark or agent that initiates transformation, while remaining unchanged, providing stability amidst flux.

- **Bridge between Opposites**: The catalyst exists in the space between forces (e.g., conflict and resolution, fear and courage, idea and action).
- **Transformation without Loss**: It does not merge into the outcome but enables it, allowing both sides of the duality to evolve.
- **Example in Life**: Insight during meditation may shift anxiety into clarity. The insight itself is not diminished; it can spark future transformations repeatedly.

Insight: Just as in chemistry, the philosophical catalyst acts silently and efficiently. It initiates change, while at the same time preserving its own presence, enabling continuous transformation.

3.Why This Matters for Life

Understanding this principle helps us recognize that catalysts are:

- **Infinite in Potential**: A single insight, idea, or action can catalyze multiple transformations.
- **Sustainable**: They don't deplete themselves; they can be engaged repeatedly.
- **Hidden yet Powerful:** Often subtle, they operate behind the scenes, yet their impact is profound.

The catalyst, whether in a chemical reaction, a moment of insight, or a creative spark, transforms without being consumed. It exists as the enduring Third, the hidden force that turns potential into reality. Tension into resolution. Duality into wholeness.

The Law of Three: Catalyst for Thought, Creation, and Balance

The Law of Three is not just a mystical principle; it is a living framework for understanding and engaging with the world. At its core, it functions as a catalyst, bridging dualities and enabling transformation in thought, creation, and balance.

1.Thought

Our minds are constantly navigating opposites: doubt and certainty, logic and intuition, fear and courage. Alone, these forces create tension or paralysis. Butwith the Third, they emerge as insight, perspective, or reflection, a catalyst that:

- Resolves Mental Conflict.
- Bridges Opposing Ideas.
- Enables Clarity and Innovation.

Example: A writer torn between two plot directions may experience a third idea, a sudden insight that reconciles the tension and brings the story to life. The Law of Three catalyzes thought by transforming duality into understanding.

2.Creation

Every act of creation, be it art, invention, problem-solving, or any other, requires the interplay of forces: Inspiration, skill, and the catalytic Third.

The Third:

- Converts potential into tangible outcomes.

- Harmonizes opposing elements to produce something new.

- Serves as the invisible spark that activates flow.

Example: A musician combines rhythm (first force) and melody (second force). The Third, harmony or silence, unifies the elements into a complete, moving composition.

3.Balance

Life itself is a dynamic system of opposing forces: Work and rest, giving and receiving, action and reflection. The Third acts as a balancing catalyst, mediating extremes and creating equilibrium.

- **In Relationships**: Empathy or compromise balances conflicting needs.

- **In Personal Growth**: Reflection or mindfulness harmonizes ambition and fear.

- **In Nature**: Predator, prey, and environment create ecological stability.

Insight: Without the Third, dualities remain in conflict. But with it, tension transforms into balance and flow.

The Law of Three as a Universal Catalyst

Across thought, creation, and balance, the Law of Three operates as a universal catalyst:

- Bridging Dualities to Unlock Insight.
- Igniting Creativity by Harmonizing Opposing Forces.
- Maintaining Equilibrium in Life, Relationships, and Nature.

The Law of Three is the hidden spark that catalyzes understanding, manifests creation, and sustains balance. Recognizing it allows us to step into life consciously, engaging the Third wherever tension exists, and transforming it into wholeness.

The Law of Three is more than a concept; it is a living catalyst. It operates silently yet powerfully, bridging dualities, sparking creation, and restoring balance. The Third is always present, in thought, guiding insight; in creation, igniting innovation; in life, harmonizing opposing forces.

Catalysts, like the Third, transform without being consumed. They exist in the space between tension and resolution, potential and reality, conflict and understanding. Recognizing the Third allows us to step consciously into the flow of life, engaging its hidden power to transform ideas, relationships, and experiences.

By observing the interplay of One, Two, and Third in our minds, in our work, and in our lives, we learn to:

- See the hidden patterns beneath all things.
- Harness the spark that turns potential into reality.
- Balance opposing forces, achieving wholeness in thought, creation, and action.

The Catalyst Principle teaches that transformation is not always a matter of force or struggle. It is a matter of attuning to the hidden spark, the Third, and allowing it to guide change naturally, gracefully, and effectively.

The Law of Three is ever-present. The question is not whether it exists. The question is whether you will recognize and engage the Third, stepping consciously into the rhythm of creation, insight, and balance.

Chapter 3

The Cosmic Triad

Chapter 2 showed us how the Third operates as a catalyst in thought, creation, and daily life. Now, chapter 3 invites us to look outward and upward; to see how the Law of Three manifests across the cosmos. The pattern is not only within us; it is woven into the very structure of reality, from the smallest atom to the largest galaxy.

The Cosmic Triad reveals how three forces, often unseen, often subtle, shape the universe:

1. **Creation**: The emergence of form and life from potential.
2. **Sustenance**: The balance that maintains structure and order.
3. **Transformation**: The force that dissolves, renews, and catalyzes evolution.

These forces exist everywhere, in cycles of stars, planetary systems, and cosmic energy. They also appear in the rhythms of nature, the dance of ecosystems, and the rise and fall of civilizations. Recognizing the Cosmic Triad allows us to see the same pattern at every scale, understanding that the Third is not only a personal or mystical principle, it is a universal law of existence.

1.Cosmic Creation

Creation is the first movement of the triad. In the universe, creation appears as the birth of stars, planets, and galaxies. Hydrogen and helium fused to form stars, atoms combined to form molecules, and energy coalesced into matter.

- In myth, this mirrors the acts of creation gods or primal forces that bring order from chaos.
- In the human mind, it mirrors ideas, intentions, and innovations emerging from raw potential.

Creation is always incomplete without the Third. Potential alone is inert; only through the catalytic force of transformation does it become manifest reality.

2.Cosmic Sustenance

The second movement, sustenance, maintains balance and continuity. Planetary orbits, ecosystems, and the cycles of life rely on equilibrium.

- **In Nature**: Predator, prey, and environment form a triadic balance.
- **In Consciousness:** Thought, feeling, and action maintain psychological harmony.

Sustenance reminds us that the universe is not static. It is a dynamic equilibrium, where the forces of creation and transformation are held in tension by the balancing Third.

3.Cosmic Transformation

The third movement is transformation, the force that dissolves, renews, and catalyzes evolution. Stars die, ecosystems evolve, civilizations rise and fall. Through transformation, the cycle continues, and growth emerges from endings.

- In myth, it appears as the gods of destruction or renewal.
- In life, it is the insight, crisis, or catalyst that triggers personal growth.

Transformation demonstrates that the Third is not destructive for its own sake. It exists to enable evolution, to turn potential and tension into new creation and balance.

4.The Triad in Natural Cycles

The Cosmic Triad repeats in nature's cycles:

- **Water**: Evaporation, condensation, precipitation.
- **Life**: Birth, growth, death.
- **Seasons**: Spring, Summer, Autumn, Winter (triads often emerge when combining the transitional stages).

These cycles illustrate that triads are not just symbolic; they are practical patterns of existence, guiding flow, adaptation, and renewal.

Reflections in Human Consciousness

The Cosmic Triad is mirrored in the human experience:

- Mind, body, spirit
- Thought, feeling, action
- Problem, conflict, resolution

The Third catalyzes understanding, harmonizes extremes, and transforms potential into reality. It is the hidden rhythm connecting personal growth to universal order.

Seeing the Universe Through the Third

When we perceive the world through the lens of the Cosmic Triad, every conflict, creation, or cycle becomes a reflection of this eternal pattern. The Third is the pulse beneath all things, quietly shaping reality across scales: Cosmic, natural, and personal.

Recognizing the Third in the cosmos allows us to see ourselves as participants, not spectators. We learn that the same principles guiding stars, atoms, and life itself guide our thoughts, actions, and relationships.

The Cosmic Triad is the universal dance of creation, sustenance, and transformation. It is the eternal pattern in which the Third, the hidden catalyst, moves everything toward balance, evolution, and wholeness.

Threefold Processes in the Universe

The universe unfolds through threefold processes, reflecting the Cosmic Triad in every scale of existence. These processes illustrate the rhythm of creation, balance, and transformation:

1.Birth: Creation

Birth is the moment when presence emerges from potential. It is creation in motion, the spark that begins a new cycle:

- **Cosmic Scale**: Stars ignite in nebulae; planets coalesce from dust and gas.
- **Natural Scale**: Seeds sprout, rivers form, ecosystems emerge.
- **Human Scale**: Ideas, projects, and intentions come into being.

Creation represents the first force, bringing latent possibilities into existence. Yet, without the subsequent forces of preservation and transformation, creation alone remains incomplete.

2.Life: Preservation

Life is the maintenance of balance, sustaining what has been created:

- **Cosmic Scale**: Gravitational forces keep planets in orbit; stars burn steadily.

- **Natural Scale**: Food chains, ecosystems, and cycles of seasons maintain equilibrium.
- **Human Scale**: Daily routines, habits, and relationships provide stability.

Preservation represents the second force, holding creation in dynamic equilibrium and allowing growth to continue. It is the ongoing pulse that sustains existence.

3.Death: Transformation/Destruction

Death is not merely an end; it is transformation, the catalyst that clears space for new creation:

- **Cosmic Scale**: As stars collapse, supernovae scatter elements for new star formation.
- **Natural Scale**: Leaves fall, animals die, and nutrients return to the soil, helping plants grow.
- **Human Scale:** Endings, failures, or crises allow reflection, hard work, growth, and renewal.

Transformation embodies the Third force, catalyzing evolution and ensuring that creation and preservation are not stagnant. Through destruction or endings, new possibilities emerge, completing the triadic cycle.

Why Threefold Processes Matter

The pattern of birth, life, and death, or creation, preservation, and destruction, is repeated universally:

- It structures the cosmos, sustaining order and evolution.
- It guides natural rhythms, ensuring adaptation and continuity.
- It mirrors human experience, helping us understand beginnings, growth, and endings as interconnected parts of a larger cycle.

The universe is a living triad. Creation sparks potential, preservation maintains it, and transformation renews it. Each process depends on the others, forming a continuous dance in which the Third, the hidden catalyst, guides the rhythm of existence.

Triads in Physics and Nature: The Third in Action

The Cosmic Triad and threefold processes, creation, preservation, and transformation, are not abstract concepts.

They appear clearly in the natural and physical world, showing how the Third functions as a hidden catalyst across scales.

1.States of Matter

Matter exists primarily in three classical states: Solid, liquid, and gas.

- **Solid (Preservation):** Stability and structure, maintaining form.
- **Liquid (Creation/Transition):** Flexibility and flow, allowing transformation.
- **Gas (Transformation/Expansion):** Freedom and dispersal, enabling renewal and change.

The Third mediates transitions, ensuring that matter evolves while maintaining continuity. The cycle of melting, freezing, and evaporation mirrors the triadic rhythm of creation, sustenance, and transformation.

2.Orbital Mechanics

Celestial bodies operate in triadic dynamics shaped by gravitational forces:

- **Planet (Creation):** Formed and positioned in a system.

- **Star/Gravity (Preservation):** Maintains orbital stability.

- **Tidal Forces/Interactions (Transformation):** Induce shifts, precession, or orbital evolution.

Here, the Third, subtle forces like tidal interactions, catalyze movement, preventing stagnation and allowing the cosmic system to evolve, demonstrating that transformation is a natural and necessary aspect of stability.

3.Ecosystem Cycles

Ecosystems follow threefold cycles that sustain life:

- **Birth/Creation**: Emergence of new species and habitats.

- **Sustenance/Balance**: Energy flows through food chains to maintain equilibrium.

- **Transformation/Death**: Decomposition, extinction, and environmental change reset the system, enabling renewal.

The Third, the transformative cycle of death and renewal, ensures resilience, adaptation, and continuity. Life thrives because the hidden force mediates balance and catalyzes evolution.

The Universal Lesson

From atoms to stars, forests to oceans, these examples illustrate a simple truth: the universe moves through triads, and the Third is the hidden catalyst that bridges duality, sparks change, and maintains flow. Recognizing these patterns helps us see the same principles mirrored in our minds, creativity, and lives, connecting cosmic, natural, and personal scales.

The states of matter, orbital mechanics, and ecosystem cycles all echo the Cosmic Triad: Creation, preservation, and transformation. The Third, the hidden catalyst, is always present, guiding evolution, sustaining balance, and activating the potential within every system.

Echoes of Triads in Human Experience

The same triadic patterns that govern stars, matter, and ecosystems also appear in the rhythms of human life. Birth, life, and death; creation, preservation, and transformation; the interplay of dualities and the Third, all are mirrored in our inner and outer experiences.

1.Thought and Creativity

- **Creation**: Ideas emerge, insights appear, and new possibilities spark.

- **Preservation**: Focus, discipline, and practice maintain and develop these ideas.

- **Transformation**: Reflection, revision, or critique transforms raw potential into meaningful results.

Example: A writer conceives a story (creation), writes and organizes it (preservation), then edits and reshapes it through feedback (transformation). The Third, insight, intuition, or a new perspective, bridges these stages, catalyzing growth and completion.

2.Emotions and Relationships

- **Creation**: Connections and feelings are born; friendship, love, empathy.

- **Preservation**: Nurturing, communication, and commitment maintain bonds.

- **Transformation**: Conflict, challenge, or change reshapes relationships, allowing them to evolve.

Example: Two colleagues in conflict may find resolution through a third perspective, mediation, shared goals, or a moment of understanding. This Third transforms tension into harmony, reflecting the same universal pattern observed in ecosystems and cosmic systems.

3.Personal Growth and Life Cycles

- **Creation**: New goals, habits, or life directions are initiated.
- **Preservation**: Daily practice, learning, and resilience sustain progress.
- **Transformation**: Challenges, failures, or transitions catalyze deeper growth and renewal.

Example: A person pursuing a career shift starts with a vision (creation), develops skills and routines (preservation), and experiences setbacks or breakthroughs (transformation). The Third, insight, support, or a shift in perspective, guides the process, just as tidal forces or decomposition guide change in the physical world.

4. Mind, Body, and Spirit

- **Mind**: Thought patterns form, stabilize, and evolve through reflection.
- **Body**: Habits and physical practices maintain health, while adaptation or challenge transforms the body.
- **Spirit**: Beliefs, intuition, and connection to purpose emerge, are nurtured, and evolve through life's trials.

The Third acts as a bridge between mind, body, and spirit, harmonizing conflicts and catalyzing growth in consciousness.

The Universal Connection

Recognizing these patterns in human experience shows that we are not separate from the cosmos. The same triads that shape matter, orbital mechanics, and ecosystems also guide our thoughts, emotions, relationships, and personal evolution. The Third, the hidden catalyst, connects dualities, sparks transformation, and sustains balance in every sphere of life.

The Cosmic Triad is not just *"out there"* in the universe; it is reflected in you. Birth, life, and death; creation, preservation, and transformation; thought, emotion, and action, all echo the eternal dance of the Third, inviting you to participate consciously in life's rhythm.

Throughout the universe, from the smallest particle to the largest galaxy, the triadic rhythm of creation, preservation, and transformation unfolds. Stars are born, planets orbit, ecosystems thrive and renew, all guided by the hidden Third, the catalyst of change.

These patterns are mirrored in human life:

- In thought and creativity, the Third sparks insight and harmonizes opposing ideas.
- In emotions and relationships, it mediates tension, enabling understanding and connection.
- In personal growth, it turns challenges into opportunities for transformation.

Physics, nature, and human experience all speak the same language: the language of triads. The Third, the unseen but ever-present catalyst, bridges dualities, initiates change, and maintains balance, connecting the cosmos with the rhythms of our daily lives.

Recognizing this pattern allows us to see that we are participants in a universal dance, not separate observers. Life is not merely a series of random events; it is a triadic flow, and the Third is the pulse that moves everything forward, shaping reality at every scale.

The Cosmic Triad reminds us that creation, preservation, and transformation are inseparable. The Third, the hidden catalyst, is always at work, inviting us to step consciously into the rhythm of the universe, align with its patterns, and harness its power in our own lives.

Part II

The Triad Within: Mind and Self

In Part I, we explored the Cosmic Triad, seeing how creation, preservation, and transformation, the Law of Three, shape the universe, natural systems, and human experience. We traced the Third, the hidden catalyst, from the birth of stars to the cycles of ecosystems, and observed its echoes in human thought, creativity, and relationships.

Now, in Part II, we turn inward, examining the triads within the mind and self, exploring how the same principles that guide the cosmos operate in our inner world. By understanding the triadic nature of consciousness, thought, emotion, and personal growth, we learn to recognize the Third within ourselves, activating insight, balance, and transformation from the inside out.

This section will guide you to:

- See how the mind itself operates through triads.
- Understand the interplay of thought, feeling, and action.

- Recognize the catalyst within, the hidden Third that bridges dualities, resolves inner conflicts, and sparks personal growth.

- Apply these insights to cultivate creativity, emotional intelligence, and self-mastery.

The universe outside and the universe within both mirror each other. The patterns we observe among stars, matter, and ecosystems are reflected in our minds, hearts, and selves. By exploring these inner triads, we step into conscious participation in the eternal dance of creation, balance, and transformation.

Chapter 4

Freud's Threefold Mind

In exploring the triads of the mind, one of the most enduring frameworks comes from Sigmund Freud's model of the psyche: The id, ego, and superego. Freud's threefold mind reflects the same underlying triadic principle we observed in the universe: A tension of forces, mediated and harmonized by an inner catalyst.

- The Id (Creation): The primal, instinctual part of the psyche, driving desire, impulse, and energy. It represents the raw, unformed potential of our inner world; our drives for pleasure, survival, and expression.

- The Ego (Preservation): The conscious self that mediates between the id and the external world, maintaining balance and adapting impulses to reality. The ego sustains structure, navigating the flow of life while protecting the integrity of the self.

- The Superego (Transformation/Third): The moral and ethical framework that shapes, refines, and elevates impulses. It introduces judgment, insight, and self-reflection, guiding the transformation and evolution of the psyche.

The Third as the Catalyst

In Freud's model, the superego functions as the Third, bridging the raw impulses of the id with the reality-based actions of the ego. It does not destroy or suppress energy but transforms it, turning potential into constructive action, insight, and moral alignment. The Third mediates conflict, catalyzes growth, and allows the psyche to function as a dynamic, evolving system.

This perspective shows that the Law of Three is not only cosmic or external, it is deeply internal, governing our thoughts, desires, and self-regulation.

Understanding the Threefold Mind provides a practical map for observing how triads operate within consciousness, offering a framework for activating the inner Third consciously.

Why This Matters

- It helps us recognize patterns of tension and mediation within our psyche.

- It reveals how personal growth often emerges from the dynamic interaction of inner forces.

- It provides a bridge between psychological theory and the mystical principle of the Third, showing how the universal law of triads applies within the self.

The id, ego, and superego illustrate the inner dance of creation, preservation, and transformation. The Third, the hidden catalyst, guides our impulses toward insight, balance, and conscious evolution.

By observing these triads, we can see how tension, energy, and insight interact in daily life.

1.Career Decisions

- **Id** (Creation): You feel a strong urge to leave a stable job and pursue a creative passion. The impulse is raw, instinctual, and filled with potential.

- **Ego** (Preservation): You weigh responsibilities, bills, family expectations, financial stability, trying your best to plan carefully.

- **Superego** (Transformation/Third): Through reflection, mentorship, or ethical consideration, a third perspective emerges, guiding you to a solution that honors both ambition and stability.

Example: You finally decide to start your passion project, working on it part-time, while maintaining your main job too, creating a pathway that transforms desire into an actionable reality.

2.Relationship Conflicts

- **Id**: During an argument, anger or jealousy surfaces. The instinctual response wants an immediate reaction.
- **Ego**: You attempt to remain calm, thinking logically about the consequences of your actions.
- **Superego** (Third): Reflection, empathy, or moral insight mediates the tension, helping you communicate constructively and find resolution.

Example: Instead of lashing out, you pause, consider your partner's perspective, and express your feelings thoughtfully, transforming conflict into understanding and growth.

3.Creative Pursuits

- **Id**: Inspiration strikes suddenly, a melody, a story idea, or a painting concept. The raw energy is full of potential but chaotic.

- **Ego**: You organize and develop the idea, applying skill and structure.

- **Superego** (Third): Intuition, critique, or aesthetic insight refines the work, harmonizing raw creativity with skill to produce a meaningful result.

Example: A songwriter experiences a burst of melody (id), brings a structure to the song and the lyrics (ego), and applies intuition and feedback to perfect the piece (superego/Third), producing art that resonates deeply.

4.Personal Growth and Habits

- **Id**: You feel the urge to procrastinate or indulge in unhealthy behaviors.

- **Ego**: You establish rules, routines, or strategies to maintain discipline.

- **Superego** (Third): Self-awareness, reflection, or insight transforms impulses into conscious choices.

Examples: Instead of succumbing to distraction, you recognize the impulse, plan a productive schedule, and transform desire into focused, disciplined action.

5.Decision-Making Under Stress

- **Id**: Panic, fear, or urgency pushes for immediate action.
- **Ego**: You assess risks, options, and consequences.
- **Superego** (Third): Inner insight, intuition, or moral reasoning provides a balanced solution, mediating instinct and logic.

Example: Facing a sudden work crisis, your first instinct might be to react impulsively (id). However, you analyze facts and deadlines (ego), and finally, an intuitive solution or calm judgment emerges (Third), resolving the situation efficiently and ethically, which could've ended in a potential conflict.

5.Learning and Education

- **Id**: Curiosity and excitement drive the desire to learn something new.

- **Ego**: Consistent study, practice, and repetition maintain progress.

- **Superego** (Third): Reflection and synthesis integrate knowledge into wisdom, connecting facts to insight.

Example: A student fascinated by science experiments (id) studies systematically (ego) and finally discovers a deeper principle or connection through reflection (Third), turning learning into understanding.

6.Social and Moral Choices

- **Id**: Immediate desire or social pressure may prompt selfish or reactive behavior.

- **Ego**: Awareness of social norms and personal goals moderates actions.

- **Superego** (Third): Conscience, empathy, or ethical insight transforms action into responsible and meaningful choices.

Example: You're tempted to gossip about a colleague (id). But awareness of fairness and professionalism (ego) guides restraint, and reflection on long-term relationships and ethics (Third) leads you to respond with integrity instead.

The Third as a Universal Catalyst

Across all these scenarios, the superego functions as the Third:

- It bridges instinct and reason.
- It transforms tension into insight.
- It allows raw energy and desire to become constructive action, creativity, or personal growth.

Recognizing and engaging the Third in everyday life allows us to navigate impulses, conflicts, and challenges consciously, turning the Law of Three from an abstract principle into a practical tool for self-mastery.

The id, ego, and superego illustrate that our inner world mirrors the universal triad. Every desire, challenge, and creative impulse is part of a hidden pattern, and the Third, the inner catalyst, guides us from raw potential to balanced, meaningful action.

Introduction to the Id, Ego, and Superego

At the heart of Sigmund Freud's model of the psyche lies a triad: The id, the ego, and the superego. Though born from psychology, this

framework reflects a universal pattern: Three forces in dynamic interaction, each with its own role, tension, and necessity. Freud did not speak in mystical terms, but his vision resonates with the

archetypal Law of Three.

The Id: The Raw Impulse (Creation)

The id is the seat of primal energy: Hunger, desire, pleasure, and instinct. It operates according to the

> *"pleasure principle,"* seeking immediate satisfaction without concern for consequences. It is the spark, the raw creative force within us.

The Ego: The Mediator (Preservation)

The ego develops as we engage with reality. It seeks balance between the impulsive drives of the id and the demands of the external world. Guided by the *"reality principle,"* it negotiates, restrains, and organizes, ensuring survival and social harmony.

The Superego: The Inner Voice (Transformation, the Third)

The superego emerges as the voice of conscience, ideals, and values. It is shaped by parents, culture, and inner reflection. Beyond mere restraint, it often catalyzes transformation, turning instinct into purpose, desire into discipline, and conflict into growth.

Together, these three elements form a living triad within the human psyche. The id supplies raw energy, the ego maintains balance, and the superego catalyzes growth, nudging us toward ethical, creative, and conscious living.

This is not only a psychological theory, but also a mirror of cosmic law: Wherever there are three, there is a cycle of energy, mediation, and transformation.

In the following sections, we will see how this inner triad plays out in everyday life, through choices, conflicts, creativity, and growth, showing how the Third operates as a catalyst within us.

How These Forces Interact: Tension, Resolution, and Balance

The triad of id, ego, and superego is not static; it is alive, constantly in motion. These three forces create an inner dialogue, sometimes harmonious, sometimes conflicting, but always shaping who we are.

- ### Tension

The id pushes with primal energy: "*I want it now.*" The superego pulls with conscience: "*You must rise above that.*" But the ego stands between them, caught in the tug-of-war of id and superego. This tension is not a flaw but a necessary friction. Without it, there would be no growth, no refinement, and no awakening of choice.

- ### Resolution

The ego, as mediator, seeks resolution by balancing desire with consequence, instinct with morality, passion with responsibility. Sometimes this means compromise, while other times, transformation. The resolution does not erase the tension, but channels it into a higher form.

- ## Balance

True balance emerges when the Third, the superego's catalytic insight, transforms the clash into harmony. What once felt like conflict between *"what I want"* and *"what I should do"* becomes a creative path forward. Balance is not a frozen stillness but a living rhythm, like walking, like a stream, constant shift between imbalance and correction that carries us forward.

An Everyday Example

Imagine a student tempted to cheat on an exam.

- The id says: "Do it. It's easy, and you'll get what you want."
- The superego says: "That's wrong. You must act with integrity."
- The ego is caught in tension, weighing the risks, consequences, and goals.

The resolution may come through the ego choosing not to cheat, honoring both personal success and moral integrity. In that moment, balance is achieved, not by silencing one force, but by letting the triad move through tension into transformation.

The Pattern Beneath

This interaction reflects the Law of Three:

- The id is the driving force (affirmation).
- The superego is the restraining force (negation).
- The ego is the reconciling force (the Third).

Together, they form a cycle of energy that mirrors the very structure of existence, conflict giving rise to growth, tension giving way to balance, and raw impulses refined into conscious life.

A Day in the Life: The Triad at Work

Meet Amara, a young professional, whose inner world reflects the same triadic pattern that lives in all of us.

Morning: Battle with the Alarm Clock

The alarm rings at 6:30 a.m.

- **Id**: "Stay in bed. Sleep feels good. Forget responsibilities."

- **Superego**: "You must wake up now. Discipline is everything. Only lazy people sleep in."

- **Ego**: Amara, while in her sleep, hesitates, torn between comfort and obligation. After a few moments, she decides to rise, but with a compromise. Five more minutes of rest, then up. Balance achieved through small negotiation.

Midday: The Temptation of Food

At lunch, a coworker brings donuts.

- **Id**:"Yes! Sugar, pleasure, eat as much as you can."

- **Superego**: "No. Donuts are unhealthy. A disciplined person would avoid them completely."

- **Ego:** The tension is strong, but the ego finds a middle path. Amara takes one donut and balances it with a salad for lunch. The pleasure is honored, but within reason.

Afternoon: Ethical Dilemma at Work

A project report is due. Amara realizes a shortcut could save time, but it would misrepresent the data.

- Id:"Do it. No one will know. You'll complete a day's work in an hour, making you look good in front of your boss."

- Superego: "That's dishonest. Integrity matters more than appearances. Never compromise your values."

- **Ego**: The stress rises as Amara weighs career advancement against ethical truth. The catalyst emerges, and her conscience reminds her of the long-term vision she holds of being respected, not just promoted. Thus, she chooses honesty, even though it's harder and requires more effort.

Here, the superego transforms the conflict, catalyzing growth. The decision strengthens her self-respect and aligns her life with the values she holds in her heart.

Evening: Creative Release

At home, Amara feels the urge to write in her journal.

- **Id**:"Write freely. Let it all pour out, uncensored."

- **Superego**: "Make it perfect, polished, worthy of sharing."

- **Ego**: Now, Amara feels blocked until she allows both forces to play. She begins writing freely (id's raw energy) and later edits a few passages (superego's refinement). The result is balance: Expression that is both authentic and meaningful.

As the day comes to an end, Amara realizes that her choices weren't about silencing any part of herself, but about allowing the three forces to converse. Each tension, between comfort and discipline, pleasure and restraint, ambition and integrity, became an opportunity to grow.

Amara's day reveals that we live in constant triads. The id provides the fuel, the superego the vision, and the ego the path that brings all of them together. This dance of tension, resolution, and balance is not a battle to be won, but a rhythm to be understood.

When we listen to these voices not as enemies but as collaborators, we discover the catalyst of the Third: A more profound wisdom that turns conflict into clarity, chaos into creativity, and desire into transformation.

Misconceptions about Them Being *"Good"* or *"Bad."*

This is crucial because many readers instinctively label the id as *"bad"* and the superego as *"good."* In reality, both are essential parts of the psyche, each playing a necessary role in maintaining balance, growth, and psychological wholeness.

Misconceptions: Good vs Bad

When people first encounter Freud's triad, they often slip into moral judgments:

- The id is dismissed, labeled as "animalistic, selfish, or bad."
- The superego is praised as "noble, moral, or good."
- The ego is seen as a referee caught in the middle. This is an oversimplification, and a dangerous one.

The Id is Not Evil

The id is the wellspring of life itself. It is the source of creativity, passion, and drive. Without it, there would be no hunger to fulfill, no desire to love, and no impulse to create art or music. To deny the id is to deny the fire that animates existence. What is *"dangerous"* is not the id itself, but when it is left unchecked, like raw energy without direction.

The Superego is Not Purely Good

The superego embodies conscience, ideals, and cultural values. Yet, sometimes it can also become harsh, rigid, or punishing. An overactive superego can drive a person into guilt, shame, or perfectionism. In such cases, what appears *"good"* can become destructive, suffocating the spontaneity of life.

The Ego is Not Weak or Neutral

The ego is sometimes misunderstood as a passive referee. In truth, it is the artist of balance, the one who draws resolution from tension, solution from a conflict. The ego is where wisdom emerges, not by suppressing either side, but by listening and weaving their energies together.

A Living Trinity, Not a Battle of Morals

To label one force "*bad*" and another "*good*" is to miss the deeper truth. Each plays its role:

- The id fuels life (raw energy).
- The superego refines life (vision and ideals).

- The ego harmonizes life (balance in action).

When they are seen not as enemies but as collaborators, their tension becomes creative, rather than destructive.

The lesson is this: The triad within us is not a war of good versus evil; it is a dance of forces, each necessary, each incomplete without the others. To live fully is not to suppress one side, but to integrate them into a higher harmony.

Chapter 5

The Inner Dance of Three

Inside every human being, a silent choreography unfolds. The id surges with desire, the superego calls with ideals, and the ego moves between them like a dancer, shaping steps that keep us upright. This is not a static system but a dance of energies, sometimes chaotic, sometimes graceful, but always alive.

In this dance:

- The id drums the primal beat, reminding us of hunger, lust, pleasure, and survival.
- The superego plays the higher melody, carrying the voice of conscience, culture, and aspiration.
- The ego listens to both rhythms, weaving them into steps that allow us to walk in the world without falling.

This is not a struggle of enemies, but a performance of balance. Like a trio of musicians, each part alone is incomplete. Together, they create harmony, or dissonance, depending on how well we listen.

The Law of Three reveals itself again: Two forces in opposition generate tension, but the third brings a balance, a transformation. Without the ego's mediation, the id's fire could consume us, or the superego's rigidity could freeze us. But when the three move together, life flows with rhythm, meaning, and balance.

To live consciously is to learn this dance, stepping not with fear or repression, but with awareness.

In the pages ahead, we will explore how this inner dance reveals itself in relationships, creativity, conflict, and healing, and how, by attuning ourselves to its rhythm, we can transform tension into harmony, chaos into clarity, and desire into purposeful action.

The Psychological Balance: A Three-Way Negotiation

Imagine, for a moment, that within you sits a round table where three

voices gather. They do not always agree, but each has power, each has purpose, and each has a say. This is the inner council of the psyche:

- The Id is the passionate negotiator. It leans forward, impatient, demanding pleasure, comfort, and immediate satisfaction. Its voice is raw and urgent: *"I want this now."*

- The Superego sits tall and stern, armed with rules, values, and visions of perfection. Its voice is lofty and absolute: *"You must do what is right, no matter the cost."*

- The Ego sits between them, listening carefully. It is not swayed by impulse or rigidity alone, but acts as a mediator. Its voice is practical: *"Let us find a way forward that both honors desire and respects principle."*

This three-way negotiation is the essence of psychological balance. It is not about silencing one voice over the other, but about allowing each to contribute to the decision-making process.

How the Negotiation Works in Daily Life

- When the id dominates, decisions feel reckless; pleasure without foresight, action without consequence.

- When the superego dominates, life becomes rigid; rules without joy, morality without compassion for human weakness.

- When the ego mediates, balance emerges; pleasure honored within limits, ideals pursued with compassion, and reality embraced with clarity.

The Catalyst of the Third

Every negotiation requires tension between two poles to generate a creative third way. The id and superego provide the push and pull, and the ego creates the synthesis. In this way, balance is not compromised in the sense of *"losing something,"* but transformed in the sense of finding a higher path that neither extreme alone could fully see.

The Dance, Not the War

Too often, people experience these voices as a battlefield: Indulgence versus guilt, freedom versus duty. But what if we saw them as dancers in negotiation, rather than soldiers at war? The ego is not a weary referee but a skilled choreographer, turning conflict into rhythm, and rhythm into harmony.

The inner negotiation is the Law of Three at work within us: One voice proposes, another opposes, and the third reconciles into a living balance. This is the dance that keeps us human, messy, imperfect, but always capable of transformation.

Real-Life Negotiations of the Inner Three

1.The Dessert at Midnight

You've finished dinner, and by midnight, the fridge seems to be calling you back; a slice of cake waits.

- The Id whispers: "Eat it. Life is short. You deserve this pleasure."
- The Superego scolds: "Absolutely not. Sugar at this hour is unhealthy. You must show discipline."
- The Ego mediates: "Perhaps I can enjoy a smaller slice, or choose fruit instead, honoring both satisfaction and health."

The result is not self-denial nor indulgence, but a balanced decision.

2.The Career Leap

You've been offered a high-paying job in a city far away from your family.

- The Id shouts: "Take it! Think of the money, the adventure, the new life."
- The Superego warns: "But what about loyalty? What will your family think? What if you fail? What would they do without you?"
- The Ego reflects: "Let's weigh the risk and reward. I can plan visits home, or perhaps negotiate flexible terms. How can I honor my ambition, without abandoning responsibility?"

Again, the ego doesn't erase either voice; it translates their tension into wisdom.

3.The Heated Argument

In a moment of anger, a friend says something hurtful.

- The Id pushes: "Strike back! How dare they disrespect you!"

- The Superego restrains: "Stay calm. A good person forgives and forgets. Don't stoop low."

- The Ego balances: "I need to acknowledge my hurt without exploding. Perhaps I'll wait until I've cooled down, then express my feelings with honesty."

This way, conflict becomes an opportunity for growth, rather than destruction.

Why These Negotiations Matter

In each example, we see the Law of Three unfolding:

- One pole pushes (id).

- Another resists (superego).

- The third creates balance (ego).

This is not a compromise in the sense of *"losing,"* it is a transformation in the sense of finding a wiser, more human path.

To recognize this inner negotiation is to reclaim power. Instead of being dragged blindly by impulse or paralyzed by guilt, we can step into the role of conscious mediator, an ego that dances, listens, and transforms.

Psychological Balance as a Three-Way Negotiation

At the core of the psyche, balance is never static. It is a living process, like an ongoing negotiation around an inner table where three distinct voices are present: The id, the superego, and the ego.

The Id speaks first and loudest. It represents our raw drives, the hunger for food, pleasure, comfort, power, and intimacy. It is immediate, urgent, and impulsive. Its motto is simple: *"I want."*

The Superego counters with authority. It carries the voice of morality, ideals, parental expectations, and cultural standards. Its demand is for perfection, order, and righteousness. Its motto is stern: *"You must."*

- The Ego sits between them, listening carefully, the sane voice. It understands the reality of the world, the limits of time, resources, and the consequences of actions. Its task is to reconcile the two forces without silencing either one. Its motto is pragmatic: *"Let's find a way."*

This three-way negotiation is not a battle where one wins and the others lose. Instead, it is a dynamic balance, a continuous adjustment, like a scale that never stops moving but remains upright.

The Balance in Everyday Life

1. The Temptation of Pleasure

- **Id**: *"Let's stay up all night watching movies."*
- **Superego**: *"That's irresponsible. Staying up all night is unhealthy. You must rest and show some discipline."*
- **Ego**: "I can enjoy one film and still get enough sleep."

2. The Pull of Ambition

- **Id**: "Take the job. It's exciting and pays well!"
- **Superego**: "But what about duty to family? What will people say?"
- **Ego**: "Let's weigh options carefully. I can pursue ambition while making plans to stay connected."

3. The Heat of Conflict

- **Id**: "Shout back. Don't let them disrespect you."

- **Superego**: "Be silent. A good person doesn't lose control."
- **Ego**: "I will wait, calm down, and then speak honestly about how I feel."

In each case, the ego is not erasing or suppressing; it is translating tension into action. This is the psychological balance of the three.

Why the Negotiation Matters

If the id dominates, life becomes reckless. If the superego dominates, life becomes rigid. Only when the ego mediates between the two can human beings live with both aliveness and responsibility.

This is the dance of three within the self, not a war, but a dialogue. Each voice contributes, and the ego's artful negotiation is what allows us to remain whole.

In this way, the "*Law of Three*" becomes visible in the psyche: Two opposing forces generate tension, and a third transforms the conflict into balance. To live consciously is to take our seat at that table, listening deeply, and guiding the conversation toward harmony.

The Danger of One Force Dominating the Others

The inner balance is delicate. When one voice overwhelms the others, the psyche loses its harmony, and life tips into distortion.

1. When the Id Dominates: The Tyranny of Impulse

The id, left unchecked, pulls us into a life ruled by desire. Thus, every craving demands immediate satisfaction.

- **Signs**: Impulsivity, addiction, reckless decisions, inability to delay gratification.
- **Example**: The person who spends every paycheck on pleasures without thinking about tomorrow. Excitement burns bright but is followed by regret, instability, and emptiness.
- Here, life becomes a cycle of endless hunger; an addiction that nothing can fulfill.

2.When the Superego Dominates: The Prison of Perfection

The superego, when too strong, strangles spontaneity and joy. Every action is judged, every desire condemned.

- **Signs**: Harsh self-criticism, guilt, anxiety, obsession with rules and appearances.
- **Example**: The student who studies relentlessly, not out of love for learning, but out of terror of disappointing others. Achievement is gained, but at the cost of freedom and inner peace.
- Here, life becomes rigid, cold, and joyless; an endless attempt to live up to the expectations of others; an impossible ideal.

3.When the Ego Dominates: The Illusion of Control

The ego, too, can lose balance when it forgets its mediating role and tries to dominate as the sole ruler.

- **Signs**: Over-rationalization, emotional detachment, denial of instinct and conscience alike.

- **Example**: The professional who makes every decision based only on efficiency, ignoring both the needs of the heart and the call of higher values.

Here, life becomes mechanical, clever but hollow, guided by calculation without depth.

The Lesson of Imbalance

In each case, the voice that dominates claims to offer security, pleasure, morality, or control, but instead leads to distortion.

- Too much id burns us out.
- Too much superego freezes us.
- Too much ego flattens us.

Balance does not come from silencing other voices, but from letting them speak in turn. The art of living is not only to obey one, but to let all three be heard, so that their tension can be transformed into wisdom.

Thus, the Law of Three shows itself again, reminding that no single pole can sustain life alone. True wholeness arises only when desire, conscience, and reality move together in a shared rhythm. This is the essence of psychological balance.

Awareness of the Triad and the Path to Self-Mastery

The id, ego, and superego will never disappear. They are not flaws in the human design, but essential voices of our inner symphony. The challenge is not to silence them, but to become aware of them, to recognize who is speaking at any given moment.

When we live unconsciously, we are pulled blindly by whichever voice shouts loudest. One day desire rules us, the subsequent guilt imprisons us, and the following calculation numbs us. This cycle continues over and over again. We swing from one extreme to another, never quite at peace.

But the moment we cultivate awareness, the dance changes. Awareness allows us to pause, to listen, and to see the triad at work. In that pause, we recognize:

- This is my id speaking; it wants immediate gratification.
- This is my superego speaking; it fears judgment and demands perfection.

- This is my ego speaking; trying to negotiate between them.

With awareness, we are no longer enslaved to any one force. We become the observer who holds the entire triad in view. And from that higher vantage point, we can choose restrain, rather than react.

This choice is the essence of self-mastery. It is not about repressing desire, erasing conscience, or overthinking every decision. It is about holding all three voices in awareness and guiding them toward balance. In this way, we are no longer tossed by inner conflict, but can walk with clarity, creativity, and freedom.

To master the self is not to silence the inner dance; it is to become the conductor of it.

And so, the Law of Three reveals itself again: Awareness transforms conflict into dialogue, dialogue into harmony, and harmony into mastery.

The triad does not bind us; it sets us free.

The dance of the id, ego, and superego is eternal, at times chaotic, at times graceful, but always alive. When left unnoticed, it can pull us in opposing directions. When observed with awareness, it becomes our teacher, our guide, and our source of inner power.

Every tension holds a lesson. Every conflict is an invitation. And every choice, when made from conscious meditation, strengthens the rhythm of the dance. The triad within is not a battlefield; it is a symphony, waiting for the master: You.

As we move forward into the next chapter, we will explore how these inner patterns shape our perception, creativity, and personal growth, showing that the dance of three is not only a psychological principle but a gateway to deeper insight, purposeful action, and self-realization.

Awareness transforms the triad from inner friction into inner freedom. The dance continues, but now, you are leading it.

Chapter 6

Shadow, Light, and Integration

In the inner dance of three, not all aspects of ourselves are visible in the light of day. Some dwell in the shadows, others as hidden desires, fears, unresolved conflicts, or suppressed impulses. However, most shine bright as our strengths, ideals, creativity, and wisdom. The triad of the psyche interacts with both shadow and light, and understanding this interplay is essential for conscious growth.

- The Id often carries the shadow: Instinctual drives, unacknowledged desires, impulses we are conditioned to deny. Yet, within the shadow lies energy, creativity, and vitality.

- The Superego often represents light: The ideals, conscience, and moral compass that guide us toward purpose. But when unbalanced, it can cast harsh judgment, creating guilt or shame.

- The Ego mediates the shadow and light, integrating them into conscious awareness. It does not suppress or glorify either; it recognizes value in both, seeking harmony and wholeness.

The Process of Integration

Integration is the act of acknowledging all parts of the self without fear or denial. It is the conscious embrace of the shadow alongside the light, guided by the mediating force of the ego. In practice:

1. **Recognition**: Notice your impulses, fears, desires, and ideals without judgment.
2. **Reflection**: Understand the origins, motivations, and consequences of these inner forces.
3. **Integration**: Allow each part to contribute constructively to thought, choice, and action.

When integration occurs, inner tension transforms into energy for growth. The shadow no longer sabotages, and the light no longer blinds. Both are aligned through the ego, the conscious Third, catalyzing transformation into wholeness.

A Glimpse of the Inner Triad at Work

- Shadow impulse arises: Anger at a friend.

- Light principle emerges: Desire to act with empathy.
- Ego mediates: Recognizing anger as a signal, then expressing it constructively and with clarity.

Here, the inner triad engages shadow, light, and integration; the dance is no longer chaotic but transformative.

To live consciously is to step fully into shadow and light, guided by the inner triad. The id, ego, and superego are not merely forces to manage; they are instruments of integration, creativity, and wholeness. Throughawareness, the dance becomes mastery, and the self becomes whole.

Real-Life Scenarios of Shadow and Light

1. The Shadow of Anger

- **Id (Shadow impulse)**: You feel sudden anger toward a colleague who overlooked your idea.
- **Superego (Light principle)**: You want to remain professional, maintain respect, and act ethically.
- **Ego (Mediator):** You recognize the anger as a signal of your unmet need for acknowledgment. You choose to

calmly address your colleague later, expressing your perspective without hostility.

Outcome: The shadow (anger) provides information and energy; the light (ethics) guides constructive action; the ego integrates both, preventing destruction while honoring truth.

1.The Shadow of Fear

- **Id (Shadow impulse):** Fear tells you to avoid a public speaking opportunity.
- **Superego (Light principle):** You know growth requires courage and facing challenges.
- **Ego (Medi**ator): You acknowledge the fear, prepare thoroughly, and step onto the stage anyway.

Outcome: Shadow fear becomes a teacher; the light principle inspires growth; ego transforms hesitation into confident action.

2.The Shadow of Desire

- **Id (Shadow impulse):** Desire urges indulgence in unhealthy habits; overeating, procrastination, or overspending.

- **Superego (Light principle):** Values, health, and long-term goals remind you of discipline and responsibility.
- **Ego (Mediator)**: You find a balanced approach: allowing moderate enjoyment without harming long-term well-being.

Outcome: Desire is neither denied nor unchecked. Integration converts impulse into informed choice.

Practical Exercises for Integration

Exercise 1: Shadow Observation

1 Identify one recurring impulse or fear (shadow) that you often ignore or

2 suppress.

3 Write down how the id expresses this shadow.

4 Note what the superego's guiding principle or ideal says about it.

5 Reflect on how your ego can mediate between the two; what balanced action can you take?

Exercise 2: Light Amplification

1 Identify a positive trait or value (light) you want to strengthen. It can be compassion, creativity, discipline, or any other action.

2 Observe how the id may resist or distort this light.

3 Determine how your ego can integrate this light into daily behavior.

4 Practice small, conscious steps to align your actions with this principle.

Exercise 3: Daily Triad Check-In

At the end of each day:

2. Recall a moment of tension and ask yourself, *"What did the id want?"*

3. Recall moments of guidance, *"What did the superego suggest?"*

4. Note and ask the most important question, *"How did the ego mediate?"*

Reflect on whether shadow and light were acknowledged, suppressed, or integrated.

The Transformative Power of Awareness

Through consistent observation and integration:

- Shadows lose their power to sabotage.

- Light becomes a source of genuine guidance, rather than rigid expectation.
- The ego becomes a skilled mediator, converting tension into clarity and growth.

The Law of Three unfolds in our daily life: Tension between shadow and light generates insight, and the ego catalyzes this into conscious action. The triad is no longer hidden; it becomes a tool for mastery, wholeness, and self-realization.

Jung's Perspective: Integrating the Unconscious

Carl Jung expanded upon the understanding of the human psyche by emphasizing the unconscious, the vast, hidden part of ourselves where the shadow resides, along with untapped creativity, instincts, and archetypal energies. For Jung, psychological wholeness depends on integration; bringing unconscious elements into conscious awareness, rather than repressing or denying them.

The Shadow in Jungian Terms

- The shadow consists of aspects of ourselves that we reject or fail to recognize, such as anger, jealousy, fears, or socially unacceptable impulses.

- Jung emphasized that the shadow is not inherently negative. It contains energy, creativity, and hidden potential. Denying the shadow leads to projection, inner conflict, and repetitive patterns in life.

The Process of Integration

Jung proposed that wholeness comes from:

1. **Awareness**: Recognizing the shadow's existence within the self.

2. **Acknowledgment**: Accepting it without judgment, seeing it as part of the human psyche.

3. **Synthesis**: Actively integrating the shadow with conscious thought and behavior, transforming inner tension into creativity and wisdom.

Connection to the Triad

- **Id (Shadow energy):** Jung's shadow often resonates with the unconscious impulses of the id; raw energy that must be acknowledged.

- **Superego (Light/Guidance):** Conscious ideals, values, and ethical principles act as the guiding light to direct that energy.

- **Ego (Mediator/Integrator**): The ego plays the critical role of bringing the unconscious into conscious awareness, allowing the individual to navigate life skillfully.

By integrating the unconscious, we do not suppress desire or fear, but learn from it, unlocking creativity, resilience, and self-knowledge.

Practical Example

Imagine someone who reacts with unexplained anger in social situations:

- Without integration, anger is projected outward or repressed.

- With Jungian integration, the person examines their unconscious triggers, recognizes unresolved fears or unmet needs (shadow), and consciously chooses responses aligned with both inner truth and social ethics (ego and superego working together).

Outcome: Conflict transforms into understanding, tension into insight, and the shadow becomes a source of growth.

Jung teaches us that the unconscious is not to be feared, but engaged. Integration is the art of bringing shadow and light into conscious balance; an inner alchemy where the triad becomes fully alive.

Triads in Emotional and Moral Growth

The Law of Three operates not only in thought and desire, but also deeply within our emotional and moral life. Emotions, impulses, and ethical principles form their own triadic interplay, mirroring the id, ego, and superego, offering a framework for conscious growth.

1.Emotional Growth

Emotional maturity often requires negotiating three forces:

- **Impulse/Emotion (Id):** Raw feelings arise, anger, joy, fear, or desire. These are unfiltered signals from the self and the environment.

- **Reflection/Conscience (Superego):** Inner ideals, values, or moral standards evaluate these emotions, guiding us toward constructive expression.

- **Integration/Choice (Ego):** The ego mediates, turning emotional impulses into conscious, intentional action.

Example: You feel jealousy toward a friend's success.

- **Id**:"I'm angry! It's unfair!"

- **Superego**:"Be gracious. Resentment is wrong."

- **Ego**: "I can acknowledge my feelings, understand why I feel this way, and celebrate my friend while learning from this emotion."

Through this triadic process, raw emotion becomes insight, and emotional growth occurs.

2.Moral Growth

Ethical development follows a similar triad:

- **Desire/Interest (Id):** Personal wants or needs that may conflict with ethical norms.
- **Principle/Ideal (Superego):** Societal, cultural, or spiritual standards that define what is "right."
- **Discernment/Action (Ego):** Practical wisdom that balances personal desire with moral guidance.

Example: You find a wallet on the street.

- **Id**:"Keep it. No one will know."
- **Superego**:"Return it. Integrity matters."
- **Ego**:"I will return it, but also make sure the person can be notified safely. I honor honesty without ignoring practical realities."

Through repeated triadic negotiation, moral intelligence develops, allowing us to navigate life with integrity without being rigid or impulsive.

3.Integration Across Life

- The emotional triad helps us process feelings, avoid repression, and cultivate resilience.
- The moral triad teaches ethical discernment, responsibility, and constructive decision-making.
- Both operate through tension, resolution, and balance: Raw impulse or emotion, ethical guidance, and conscious integration.

This shows that the Law of Three is not abstract; it is embedded in every act of self-awareness, emotional insight, and moral choice. The triad transforms experience into wisdom, empathy, and personal mastery.

When we understand and practice the triad within emotions and morality, we cultivate the inner tools to navigate life with clarity, balance, and integrity. The id, ego, and superego, together with shadow and light, become a living framework for growth, emotional, moral, and spiritual.

Practices for Balancing Internal Forces

Balancing the id, ego, and superego, at the same time integrating shadow and light, requires conscious attention.

The following practices provide tools to cultivate awareness, negotiation, and integration of the triad within:

1.Mindful Observation

- **Purpose**: To notice impulses, desires, judgments, and ethical considerations without immediate reaction.

- **Practice**: Spend 5-10 minutes daily observing your thoughts and emotions. Ask:
  - "What is my id wanting right now?"
  - "What is my superego advising or restricting?"
  - "How is my ego mediating between these forces?"

- **Benefit**: Awareness allows tension to become dialogue instead of conflict.

2.Shadow Journaling

- **Purpose**: To engage with unconscious or suppressed aspects of the self.

- # Practice

1. Write down recurring impulses, fears, or desires that feel uncomfortable.
2. Reflect on where these come from and what they might be signaling.
3. **Ask**: How can I integrate this energy constructively, rather than repress or act blindly?

- **Benefit**: Transform hidden or denied impulses into insight, creativity, and self-understanding.

1.Triad Reflection Before Decisions

- **Purpose**: To actively mediate between desire, principle, and reality.
- **Practice**: Before making a choice, pause and ask:
  - **Id:** What do I truly want or feel?
  - **Superego**: What do my values, ideals, or ethical standards suggest?

- Ego: How can I integrate these into a balanced decision?

- **Benefit**: Reduces impulsive mistakes and rigid moral overcorrection; Strengthens conscious self-mastery.

2.Emotional Calibration

- **Purpose**: To process emotions without suppression or overindulgence.

- **Practice**: When a strong emotion arises:

1. Label it, such as anger, fear, jealousy, joy.
2. Observe its intensity and origin (id impulse).
3. Consider ethical or value-based guidance (superego).
4. Determine a constructive action (ego).

- **Benefit**: Cultivates emotional intelligence and resilience.

3.Daily Triad Check-In

- **Purpose**: To maintain ongoing balance and awareness.

- **Practice**: At the end of each day, reflect on:
    - *"Which impulses did I notice today?"*
    - *"Where did my ideals guide me?"*
    - *"How did my ego mediate?"*
- **Benefit**: Builds a habit of conscious negotiation, turning tension into wisdom over time.

4.Integration Rituals

- **Purpose**: To align shadow, light, and conscious action.
- **Practice**: Engage in creative or reflective activities. It can be writing, art, meditation, or mindful movement, where you intentionally allow both raw impulses (shadow) and guiding principles (light) to contribute.
- **Benefit**: Encourages the triad to collaborate, strengthening harmony between internal forces.

Through these practices, the triad of id, ego, and superego transforms from becoming the source of conflict to a dynamic tool for self-mastery. Awareness, reflection, and integration turn inner tension into clarity, desire into disciplined action, and shadow into creative potential.

The journey of the self is a journey through shadow and light. Desire and principle. Chaos and clarity. Within each of us, the id, ego, and superego form a triad that pulses like a living rhythm, sometimes discordant, sometimes harmonious, but always teaching, always guiding.

Awareness is the key. When we observe the voices within, we transform tension into dialogue. When we integrate the shadow and honor the light, we cultivate emotional depth, moral discernment, and personal mastery. The inner triad is not a prison or a battlefield; it is a symphony, and the ego is the conductor.

The practices of mindful observation, shadow journaling, emotional calibration, and triad reflection allow us to step consciously into this inner dance. Through them, the Law of Three is not merely a theory; it becomes a living principle, shaping the way we feel, choose, and grow.

The triad within is both a mirror and a compass. It reflects who we are and guides us toward who we can become. To engage it consciously is to step into wholeness, transforming inner friction into wisdom and inner chaos into harmony.

As we move into the next chapter, we will explore how these inner triads extend outward, shaping our relationships, social interactions, and creative expression, showing that the dance of three is not only within us but also in the world around us.

Part III

The Law of Three in the World

Up until now, we have explored the triad as it unfolds in the cosmos and within the self. We've seen how the pattern of three moves through creation, through thought, through shadow, through light, weaving harmony from tension and meaning from chaos. But the triad does not end within us; it extends outward into the world we build together.

Every society, culture, and relationship bears the imprint of the Law of Three. It is present in the ways we structure families and communities, in the way justice is sought, in art and creativity, in science and innovation. From governments formed on checks and balances, to stories shaped around beginnings, middles, and ends, the triad whispers its design into the fabric of collective life.

Where the individual triad teaches inner balance, the worldly triad reveals relational balance; the dance of self, other, and the space between. It is here that we begin to see how the pattern beneath all things becomes the pattern between all things.

In this part of the book, we will explore how the Law of Three manifests in:

- **Relationships and Communication**: How the triad shapes the dynamics of love, conflict, and reconciliation.

- **Society and Culture**: How structures of governance, justice, and tradition reflect triadic patterns.

- **Creativity and Innovation**: How the dance of idea, process, and product mirrors the catalyst of existence.

The triad is not just a hidden pattern; it is a living architecture of connection. By recognizing it in the world around us, we learn not only to understand life more deeply, but also to participate in it more harmoniously.

Chapter 7

Three in Relationships

Every relationship is more than a dialogue; it is a triad. Whenever two people come together, a third presence arises: The relationship itself. It is the invisible thread woven between them, carrying their words,silences, emotions, and unspoken expectations.

This triadic structure appears everywhere.

In love, it becomes you, the other person, and the connection you create together. In friendship, it is you, the other person, and the bond you share.

In conflict, it is your truth, their truth, and the ground where they meet.

What may seem like a simple exchange between two becomes a dynamic balance of three.

The ancient civilizations understood this mystery. In Egyptian, Greek, and Vedic traditions alike, the power of the triad was seen as a sacred law woven into creation. Many spiritual traditions honor marriage as not just the joining of two people, but the creation of a sacred third. In modern-day psychology, therapists recognize that relationships thrive not only on individual needs but on the *"space between,"* a living field that must be nurtured as carefully as each person.

When the triad is healthy, it becomes a source of growth, intimacy, and strength. When one force overwhelms the others, when self eclipses union, or union suffocates self, the balance breaks, and the dance falters.

In this chapter, we will explore:

- The triadic structure of love and connection.
- Conflict as a threefold process: hurt, dialogue, reconciliation.
- How awareness of the *"third"* transforms relationships into spaces of growth.

To see relationships through the lens of three is to recognize that we are never alone in them; we are constantly co-creating a living presence that reflects, tests, and shapes us.

The Triad of Love: Self, Other, and Union

Consider a couple, Maya and David.

- Maya values independence and needs space to pursue her passions.

- David longs for closeness and feels most secure when they share time together.

At first glance, their desires pull in opposite directions. But when they begin to see their relationship as a triad, a shift occurs. They realize it is not only Maya's needs or David's needs that matter, but also the health of the union they've created together.

By asking, *"What does our relationship need?"* they discover a balance: Time apart for self-growth, time together for intimacy, and a shared commitment to the bond itself. In this way, the triad transforms tension into harmony.

The Triad of Conflict: My Truth, Your Truth, and Reconciliation

Conflict, too, follows the Law of Three.

Imagine two colleagues, Aisha and Luis, who find themselves at odds over a project.

- Aisha's truth: She believes efficiency comes first.

- Luis's truth: He values creativity, even if it takes longer.

If each holds only to their own position, the relationship strains. But the triadic path invites a third force: Reconciliation. This is not a compromise in the sense of loss, but the creation of something new, perhaps a method that balances efficiency and creativity.

Here, the triad becomes a catalyst, transforming conflict into collaboration.

The Triad of Friendship: You, the Other Person, and the Bond You Share

Friendship offers another example. Think of two close friends, Elena and Joy. Their connection has lasted for years because they both honor not just each other, but the friendship itself.

- When one is busy, the other is patient, knowing the bond is bigger than a single season of absence.

- When disagreements arise, they protect the friendship first, asking, *"What will keep our bond alive?"*

By nurturing the third presence, which is the living bond between them, their friendship becomes resilient, weathering the tests of time.

In every relationship, the Law of Three is quietly at work. To honor self, other, and the bond is to create connections that are not only alive but life-giving.

How Triadic Patterns Shape Communication and Conflict.

The Triad of Communication: Speaker, Listener, and Meaning

Every act of communication is more than words exchanged. It is a triadic dance of:

1. **Speaker:** The one expressing thought or emotion.
2. **Listener**: The one receiving and interpreting.
3. **Meaning:** The third presence that arises in the space between them.

When communication falters, it's often because one part of the triad is mostly neglected.

- If the speaker dominates (talking without listening), the balance breaks.
- If the listener fails to engage (hearing but not truly receiving), meaning is lost.
- If meaning is ignored (both speak but fail to connect), the conversation becomes empty.

Healthy communication arises when all three are honored. The speaker is clear, the listener is present, and both attend to the meaning that emerges beyond their individual words.

The Triad of Conflict: Assertion, Response, and Resolution

Conflict also unfolds in three phases:

1. **Assertion**: One voice expresses its truth, need, or wound.

2. **Response**: The other reacts, offering their truth or the counterpoint.

3. **Resolution**: The third way appears to be a ground where both truths can coexist or evolve into something new.

For example, in a family disagreement:

- A teenager asserts independence, "I need freedom to make my own choices."

- The parent responds with concern, "I need to know you're safe."

- Resolution arises not by erasing either need, but by creating a balanced third path, something like agreed boundaries that allow the freedom their kid wants, while at the same time ensuring their safety.

Without resolution, conflict loops endlessly between assertion and response. In this way, the triad acts as a catalyst, preventing the cycle from collapsing into stalemate.

In communication and conflict, the Law of Three acts as a hidden guide. It teaches us that real connection is not about winning or losing, but about creating a living third space where understanding, growth, and reconciliation can be born.

The Role of the Third Element in Resolving Tension

In every moment of tension, whether between lovers, friends, family, or colleagues, two forces stand face to face. One says, *"This is my truth."* The other answers, "This is mine." If the exchange ends there, the conflict becomes a battle of wills, pushing both sides into resistance, regardless of which perspective is actually true.

The Law of Three teaches us that resolution comes not from one side overpowering the other, but from the emergence of a third element, a new possibility that honors both while transcending them.

- In relationships, this third element is the bond itself. When two people shift their focus from *"me versus you"* to *"what keeps our relationship whole?"*, new solutions appear.

- In dialogue, the third element is shared meaning. Misunderstanding dissolves when both attend not only to speaking and listening, but to what is being created in between.

- In conflict, the third element is reconciliation, not a bland compromise, but a transformation that integrates opposing truths into a more expansive whole.

The third element is like a hidden doorway. It cannot be forced, but it appears when both sides pause, listen, and allow something larger than themselves to enter the space. It is the catalyst of balance; the invisible bridge between tension and harmony.

To embrace the third element is to recognize that we are not locked in duality. Between every *"you"* and *"me"* lies a living third presence; an ally that guides us toward growth, resolution, and deeper connection.

Let's look at this through an example:

Elena and Marcus had been married for seven years when their relationship started to crack.

- Elena longed for adventure: Travel, new projects, the thrill of change.

- Marcus craved stability: Routine, financial security, and a quiet home life. Their conversations often turned into the same loop:

- Elena accused Marcus of holding her back.

- Marcus accused Elena of being reckless.

Two forces pulling in opposite directions, locked in a tug-of-war. The more each defended their position, the further apart they drifted.

One evening, exhausted from yet another argument, Elena sighed and said, *"We can't go on like this. I don't want to lose us."* Marcus, equally tired, whispered, *"Neither do I."*

And in that moment, the third element quietly entered the room: The relationship itself.

Instead of debating who was right, they began to ask a new question: *"What does our marriage need?"* That shift changed everything.

Through this third path, they discovered that the marriage needed both adventure and security, but in balance. So, they made a plan: each year, they would set aside money for a big trip (feeding Elena's need for novelty), while also committing to a stable savings plan (honoring Marcus's need for safety).

While the tension did not vanish overnight, however, something deeper was born: A recognition that beyond her truth and his truth lived their shared truth.

The third element had done its quiet work, turning conflict into collaboration, and protecting the bond they both feared losing.

The third element does not erase difference; it transforms it. Where duality breeds division, the triad creates wholeness. In every relationship, it is the invisible bridge that carries us from tension to trust.

Triads in Family Dynamics, Leadership, and Creativity

Triads in Family Dynamics

Families naturally form triads, and these patterns often determine harmony or tension.

- In a parent-parent-child triad, the child often acts as the *"third element,"* balancing or absorbing tensions between parents. Healthy families recognize this and avoid placing the child in the role of mediator.

- In sibling relationships, a third sibling can soften rivalry between two, sparking a creative alliance.

- In extended families, grandparents often play the role of the wise *"third presence,"* bridging generational gaps between parents and children.

When the triad is healthy, love flows in all directions. But if one role dominates, let's say, when parents use a child as a confidant, the triad distorts, leaving an imbalance.

Through awareness, we can restore the natural balance where each voice has its place and is heard.

Triads in Leadership

Leadership, too, follows the rhythm of three. Every leader must negotiate between:

1. **Vision**: The dream or goal they are reaching toward.

2. **People**: The community or team they are guiding.

3. **Reality**: The practical constraints of resources, time, and circumstances.

A visionary who ignores people becomes a dictator. A people-pleaser who ignores vision drifts without direction. A realist who clings only to limitations stifles growth.

But when vision, people, and reality move together, leadership transforms into inspiration. Great leaders are those who can weave these three into harmony, creating progress that feels both grounded and alive.

Triads in Creativity

Every act of creation is born from a triad:

1. **Inspiration**: The spark, the raw idea, that one dream.

2. **Discipline**: The structure, the practice, the steady hand that shapes the work.

3. **Flow**: The living energy that moves between inspiration and discipline, making the process joyful and alive.

An artist who only waits for inspiration may never complete their work. One who only clings to discipline may lose vitality and originality. The dance of creativity requires all three. Inspiration ignites, discipline anchors, and flow unite them into a living work of art.

Family, leadership, and creativity each reveal the Law of Three at work. In every sphere of life, the triad reminds us that wholeness is not found in duality, but in the living third presence that balances, bridges, and transforms.

Whether in family, leadership, or creativity, the pattern is clear: Life resists the flatness of two. Wherever there is tension between opposites, a third force waits to emerge, not as a mere compromise, but as a living bridge.

In families, it is the child who embodies love beyond parental differences. In leadership, it is the vision that unites people with reality.

In creativity, it is the flow, the current that carries inspiration into form.

The mystics have long said: *"Where two are gathered, the Third is present."* This third is not visible to our naked eyes, but it is always felt. It is the quiet catalyst of balance; the hidden force that keeps love from shattering, dialogue from breaking, and creation from dissolving.

To see relationships through the lens of three is to honor their sacred depth. No bond is simply "*me*" and "*you*," it is also the mystery between us, the third element that makes connection possible.

And so, the Law of Three teaches us that in every human bond, wholeness comes not from one voice winning over the other, but from the emergence of a third, higher harmony that holds all things together.

Chapter 8

Three in Society and History

Societies, like individuals, are living systems shaped by tension, balance, and resolution. History itself is a story of triads; cycles of power, culture, and conscience that rise, clash, and transform. Just as the triad within the self fosters growth, so do the triads within society catalyze progress, conflict, and renewal.

At the heart of every social system lies a recurring pattern of three:

1. **Authority**: The structures and leaders who guide, enforce, and create order.

2. **People**: The collective energy, needs, and voices of the population.

3. **Ideals or Principles**: The moral, philosophical, or spiritual vision that directs both authority and society.

When these three forces are aligned, societies thrive. When one dominates the others, instability, oppression, or collapse can follow. History is full of such lessons: Empires, democracies, and revolutions all demonstrate the Law of Three in action.

In this chapter, we will explore how triads manifest across:

- **Governance and Political systems**: Authority, people, and principles in tension and balance.
- **Cultural Evolution**: The interplay of art, belief, and tradition.
- **Historical Movements**: The triad of awareness, action, and transformation that drives societal change.

By seeing history through the lens of three, we gain not only insight into the past but guidance for shaping the future. Societies, like individuals, are alive in triads, and understanding these patterns illuminates the hidden architecture beneath all human events.

How Civilizations Use Triads for Governance and Law Triad in Governance and Law

Civilizations throughout history have instinctively used triads to maintain balance, prevent concentration of power, and ensure justice. The triadic pattern appears across authority, the governed, and guiding principles.

1. The Three Branches of Government

- **Legislative**: Creates laws that reflect societal needs and ideals.
- **Executive**: Enforces laws and implements policy.
- **Judiciary**: Interprets laws, ensures fairness, and restrains excess.

Example: In the United States, this triad prevents any single branch from dominating. The checks and balances system is a classic embodiment of the Law of Three: Tension exists, but resolution is achieved through interaction, stability, and adaptability.

2. Historical Civilizations

- **Ancient Rome**: The Consuls, Senate, and People formed a triad balancing executive power, representative governance, and popular sovereignty.

Each element acted as a check on the others, preventing tyranny.

- **Medieval England:** The Monarch, Nobility, and Commoners created a dynamic tension that allowed the gradual evolution of law, such as the Magna Carta, balancing authority, privilege, and the rights of the people.

3. Triads in Legal Philosophy

- **Law, Justice, and Morality**: Across cultures, codified rules alone do not suffice.
    - Law establishes norms.
    - Justice ensures fairness in applying the law.
    - Morality provides the guiding principle that informs both law and justice.

Example: In Islamic jurisprudence, Sharia integrates Quranic principles (ideals), judges' rulings (interpretation), and societal needs (practical application); a triadic system ensuring laws are ethical, flexible, and socially relevant.

4. Modern Applications

- **Corporate Governance**: Board of Directors (decision-making authority), Shareholders (stakeholders' interests), and Ethics/Compliance frameworks (principled guidance) form a triad that prevents abuse and encourages sustainable growth.

- **International Law**: Nations, International Organizations (e.g., UN), and Treaties create a triad that maintains balance between sovereignty, collective action, and ethical standards.

Across time and cultures, civilizations have recognized, often intuitively, that duality alone cannot sustain governance. Only the triad, the interaction of authority, people, and guiding principle, creates a living, adaptable, and just system.

The Nigerian Governance Triad

In Nigeria, the interplay between Leadership, Citizens, and Ethical Principles forms a dynamic triad that shapes the nation's governance landscape.

- **Leadership**: Elected officials and public servants who hold decision-making power.

- **Citizens**: The populace that engages in civic duties, voting, and holding leaders accountable.

- **Ethical Principles**: Foundational values such as justice, transparency, and the rule of law that guide governance.

Illustrative Example: The Nigerian Economic Summit Group (NESG)

The NESG exemplifies a collaborative approach where the triadic model is in action:

- **Leadership**: The Nigerian Governors' Forum (NGF) represents the executive arm of the government.

- **Citizens**: The NESG acts as a bridge, representing the interests of the private sector and civil society.

- **Ethical Principles**: The NESG promotes policies grounded in sustainable development and ethical governance.

Through initiatives like the NESG/NGF Economic Roundtable, these three forces collaborate to address economic challenges, demonstrating how the triad can lead to effective governance and policy-making.

The United States' Checks and Balances

The US Constitution was designed around a triadic system: Legislative, Executive, and Judicial.

- Legislative (Congress) drafts laws reflecting the will of the people.
- Executive (President) implements and enforces laws.
- Judiciary (Supreme Court) interprets laws and ensures fairness.

When President Truman attempted to seize steel mills during the Korean War, the Supreme Court intervened, demonstrating the triad at work. Tension arose; the third element, the judiciary, restored balance, preserving democratic order. In this way, the triadic system prevents tyranny and fosters adaptability over time.

Ancient Rome

The Roman Republic exemplifies a triad balancing power:

- **Consuls**: Two executives sharing authority, preventing one from dominating.

- **Senate**: Representatives of Rome's elite, providing governance wisdom and oversight.

- **People (Assemblies)**: Representing citizens' voice, influencing decisions through voting.

Conflicts were inevitable, but the triad created mechanisms for resolution. Law like the Twelve Tables emerged from negotiation among the three elements, demonstrating how tension catalyzed enduring legal structures.

India's Constitutional Democracy

India's governance triad reflects a balance of Parliament, Judiciary, and Executive, layered with Principles of Justice derived from its Constitution.

- Landmark cases, such as Kesavananda Bharati v. State of Kerala (1973), illustrate the triad. Parliament sought to amend laws, but the Supreme Court interpreted constitutional limits, protecting democratic ideals.

- The people, through civic engagement, voting, and activism, form the third living element, ensuring the law evolves without losing its ethical grounding.

International Governance: The UN

The UN International Law operates through a triad:

- **Nations**: Exercise sovereignty and pursue national interests.

- **International Organizations** (UN, ICC): Mediate, set standards, and foster cooperation.

- **Treaties and Ethical Norms**: Provide guiding principles ensuring justice, peace, and accountability.

Conflicts, such as the disputes in the South China Sea, are managed through this triad. No single force dictates outcomes; balance emerges from negotiation among all three.

These cases demonstrate that triads are not abstract; they are practical, life-saving mechanisms. Across history and geography, societies that embrace triadic structures in governance, law, and ethics achieve stability, adaptability, and justice. The tension among the three forces is not a problem; it is the engine of civilization.

Examples from art, architecture, and culture Triads in Art

Art often unfolds in threes, whether in composition, theme, or interpretation:

- **Visual Arts**: Many classical paintings use a triangular composition to create balance and focus. For example, Leonardo da Vinci's The Last Supper places Jesus and key apostles in a triangular arrangement, drawing the eye naturally to the central figure.

- **Literature**: Stories frequently follow a three-act structure, the beginning, middle, and end, creating narrative tension and resolution. Shakespeare's plays and African folktales alike rely on this triadic rhythm.

- **Music**: Triads in harmony (three-note chords) are the foundation of Western music, producing consonance and emotional depth. African drumming often layers three rhythmic patterns to create complex, dynamic textures.

Triads in Architecture

Buildings and monuments use triads to embody stability, symbolism, and aesthetic harmony:

- **Pyramids and Temples**: Ancient Egyptian pyramids and many sacred structures use three-part designs, base, body, apex, to symbolize earthly, intermediate, and divine realms.

- **Modern Architecture**: In civic spaces, a triad of form, function, and environment guides design. For example, Lagos' National Theatre balances structural integrity (function), aesthetic impact (form), and cultural context (environment).

- **Sacred Spaces**: Many African shrines and communal halls incorporate triadic spatial arrangements to reflect spiritual, social, and cultural hierarchies.

Triads in Culture

Cultural expressions such as rituals, festivals, and belief systems often rely on threefold patterns:

- **Festivals**: Traditional Nigerian festivals, like the New Yam Festival of the Igbo people, balance community celebration, spiritual thanksgiving, and agricultural renewal. The triad sustains cohesion and meaning.

- **Folktales and Proverbs**: Many African stories use three trials, three characters, or three journeys to teach lessons, embed values, and maintain narrative rhythm.

- **Cultural Practices**: Daily life often revolves around triads: Work, rest, and celebration; or family, community, and spiritual devotion, reflecting the Law of Three in lived experience.

In art, architecture, and culture, triads are more than patterns; they are the principles of harmony, balance, and meaning. Across civilizations, threefold structures guide perception, experience, and memory, reflecting a hidden architecture that connects the personal, social, and cosmic.

Across time and space, triads have shaped the foundations of human life. In governance, they balance authority, people, and ethical principles.

In history, they drive transformation through tension, action, and resolution. In art, architecture, and culture, they create harmony, meaning, and resonance.

The pattern is unmistakable: duality alone, be it ruler and ruled, tradition and innovation, chaos and order, cannot sustain life, society, or culture. It is the third element, the living bridge, the hidden fulcrum, that transforms tension into stability, conflict into growth, and creativity into enduring expression.

Recognizing triads is to recognize the subtle currents that shape civilization. They are the invisible threads connecting the personal, the social, and the cosmic, reminding us that the principles guiding the self are mirrored in society, history, and culture.

The Law of Three is everywhere. In the stories we tell, the structures we build, and the societies we shape. To understand it is to perceive the hidden architecture of existence and to participate consciously in the creation of balance and harmony.

Chapter 9

The Hidden Third

Every duality demands resolution. Light and shadow, joy and sorrow, self and other, when they meet, they create tension. If the world were

built only on twos, it would collapse into endless struggle: Push against pull, rise against fall, one force locked in eternal battle with its

opposite.

But life does not remain in a stalemate. Something always emerges to reconcile the tension, to weave together the opposites into something new. This is the Hidden Third, the quiet mediator, the unseen catalyst, the principle that transforms conflict into creation.

Philosophers and mystics across cultures have spoken of this mystery:

- In alchemy, it is the philosopher's stone, the element that unites fire and water.

- In Christian theology, it is the Holy Spirit, the breath that bridges Father and Son.
- In Eastern philosophy, it is the middle path, the way that transcends extremes.
- In African cosmology, it appears as the trickster figure or mediator spirit who bridges human and divine.

The Hidden Third is not always visible. Yet, its fingerprints are everywhere: In the child born of love, in reconciliation after conflict, in the spark of inspiration that comes only when reason and passion are both exhausted. It is the invisible hand of transformation, the principle that ensures the Law of Three is not just a static pattern but a living, breathing process.

To understand the Hidden Third is to grasp the secret of creation itself: The unseen catalyst that makes life more than a series of opposing forces, and transforms existence into a dance of becoming.

The Unseen Force That Bridges Opposites

Opposites by themselves create tension, but tension alone cannot give birth to something new. A bridge is needed; a subtle, often invisible presence that allows energy to flow and transformation to occur. This is the unseen force, the *"hidden third"* that turns contradiction into wholeness.

We can think of it in many ways:

- In nature, day and night are bridged by twilight. It is neither fully light nor fully dark, but a luminous in-between that allows life to adjust and move forward.

- In relationships, when two people disagree, resolution is not found in one side winning, but in a third space, understanding each other, that transforms conflict into connection.

- In creativity, reason and imagination may seem opposed, but the true spark of innovation comes when a third element, intuition, enters, weaving logic and vision together.

- In the psyche, as Jung observed, the integration of the shadow is not achieved by denying darkness or worshiping light, but by finding a middle ground where both can coexist within the self.

This unseen force is rarely obvious because it does not seek dominance. It does not shout; it whispers.

It does not impose; it reconciles.

Its power lies in mediation, not in victory.

It is like the still point in a spinning wheel, invisible, yet holding the entire motion together.

Mystics have long recognized this hidden principle. The Taoists call it the Tao, the way that balances yin and yang. In Christianity, it is the Spirit that flows between Father and Son. In African traditions, it appears as the mediating spirit, the one who carries messages between humans and the divine.

The unseen force reminds us that life is never simply about choosing sides. Wholeness is born when opposites are brought into dialogue, when dualities are held long enough for something new to emerge. It is this mysterious third element that allows evolution, creativity, and peace to flourish.

Imagine a violin string pulled taut between two pegs. On its own, the tension is almost unbearable, tight, stretched, on the verge of snapping. Yet, when the bow draws across it, something miraculous happens: The string does not break; it sings.

The sound that arises is not the string alone, nor the bow alone; it is the meeting of tension and motion, given voice by a third presence: resonance. Without resonance, the string is only under tension. With it, that same tension becomes music.

This is the nature of the hidden Third. It is the resonance that transforms strain into harmony, conflict into growth, duality into creation. You cannot hold it in your hand or point to it directly, but you can hear it, feel it, and know it in the transformation it brings.

The unseen force is resonance itself; the mystery that allows life to turn opposites into symphonies.

- ## The Mystical Third Presence

Across spiritual traditions, the number three is never just arithmetic; it points to the presence of a mysterious force that reconciles opposites and breathes life into the whole. This third presence is often described as unseen. Yet, it is considered the most vital element of the triad.

- ## Christianity: The Holy Spirit

The Father and the Son are two distinct aspects. Yet, without the Spirit, their relationship would remain abstract. The Spirit is the living breath that unites them, the presence that bridges heaven and earth, divine and human, belief and experience.

- ## Hinduism: Brahma, Vishnu, Shiva

Creation (Brahma) and destruction (Shiva) might appear as opposites, but it is Vishnu, the preserver, who stands as the balancing third presence, holding the cosmos together so that creation and destruction do not spiral into chaos.

- ## Taoism:Tao Beyond Yin and Yang

Yin and yang dance in perpetual polarity, but the Tao is the silent third, neither yin nor yang. The Tao is the very essence that allows their harmony; the presence behind the balance, the unseen source from which both emerge.

- ## African Mysticism: The Mediator Spirit

In many African cosmologies, the human and divine exist in parallel, often too vast a distance for direct contact. Thus, the third presence emerges as a messenger or trickster spirit, one who bridges the gap. This figure holds the paradox of being neither fully divine nor fully human, yet embodying the bridge that makes communion possible.

- ### Alchemy: The Philosopher's Stone

Fire and water, sulfur and mercury, left to themselves, they oppose and cancel each other. But the alchemist sought the philosopher's stone, the third presence that unites the irreconcilable, turning conflict into transformation and lead into gold.

The mystical third is always more than balance; it is the spark of transcendence. It is the whisper of something greater that arises when opposites are held long enough for mystery to emerge.

Where two stand in opposition, the third presence descends. Where duality reigns, the third opens a doorway into wholeness.

Using the Law of Three as a Tool for Insight and Innovation

The Law of Three is not only a mystical pattern; it is also a practical tool for unlocking fresh perspectives. When we recognize that every polarity longs for a third presence, we begin to see problems, conflicts, and even creative blocks in a new light.

1. In Personal Insight:

When facing an inner conflict, such as fear versus desire, the Law of Three invites us to look for a third element: Wisdom. Fear says, *"Don't move."* Desire says, *"Leap now."* Wisdom becomes the hidden third that says, *"Move, but prepare."* By holding tension instead of forcing a choice, we allow new insight to emerge.

2. In Relationships

Arguments often trap people in two positions: *"I am right"* versus *"You are wrong."* But innovation in communication happens when both take a step back and ask, *"What deeper truth do we share?"*That shared truth, it can be respect, love, or mutual purpose, becomes the third element that transforms conflict into connection.

3. In Innovation and Creativity

Every breakthrough in history arises when two opposing forces meet and are transcended by a third:

- **Science**: wave and particle → Quantum Theory, a third model that unites them.

- **Technology**: art and engineering → Design, a third discipline that bridges them.
- **Business**: profit and ethics → Sustainability, a third path that honors both.

As a Way of Seeing:

When we practice the Law of Three, we learn to ask new questions:

- Instead of "Which side is right?" → "What is the unseen third possibility?"
- Instead of "What must I eliminate?" → "What bridge can I build?"
- Instead of "How do I win?" → "How can something new emerge from this tension?"

The Law of Three becomes a compass for insight. It teaches us that truth is rarely found in extremes, but in the subtle space between. Innovation, wisdom, and creativity live not in the clash of opposites, but in the discovery of the third path, the one that transcends both while honoring each.

In West African tradition, the talking drum is more than an instrument; it is a language. Long ago, villages often faced conflict. Hunters wanted the forest for game, while farmers wanted it to be cleared for crops. Each group stood on opposite sides, certain of their truth, thinking they were on the right.

One wise elder noticed that arguments only deepened the division. He took his drum and played a rhythm that echoed the heartbeat, *"ba-dum, ba-dum."* The hunters heard it as the call of the forest. The farmers heard it as the pulse of the earth. Both were correct, yet neither had the whole truth.

The elder said, "The drum has two skins, yet one voice. When I strike this side, it is sharp; when I strike the other, it is deep. But only together do they make a song."

From this teaching, the villagers discovered a third path: Designating land where hunting and farming could coexist, each nourishing the other. In this way, what began as conflict became innovation, guided by the unseen third.

This story mirrors what innovators across time have done:

- Steve Jobs fused art and technology to create devices that were both functional and beautiful.

- Wangari Maathai in Kenya fused ecology and community by planting trees to restore the land while empowering women.

- In daily life, we fuse intuition and logic to make wise decisions.

The Law of Three always asks: *"What is the drumbeat that unites the skins? What is the third path waiting to be heard?"*

The hidden third is not something to be seized, nor something to be forced. It moves quietly, like breath between words or light glimmering at the edge of night. It does not erase opposites, but allows them to sing together, as the bow does with the string.

Across traditions, across history, across the very fabric of nature, this third presence has always been there, bridging, weaving, transforming. We cannot always name it. Yet, when it comes, we recognize it. It is the unexpected harmony, the resonance that carries us beyond what we thought possible.

Perhaps, then, the Law of Three is not only a principle of existence but also a mystery: The reminder that between every *"yes"* and *"no,"* every beginning and end, every shadow and light, there waits an unseen force, inviting us into wholeness.

Part IV

Living the Catalyst

Up until now, we have explored the Law of Three in myth, mind, cosmos, and society. We have seen it as a pattern etched into existence itself, shaping stories, cycles, and structures across the seen and unseen world. Yet, a question rises, quietly but insistently: How do we live it?

To understand a principle is one thing; to embody it is another. The Law of Three is not only a lens for observation; it is a fire for transformation. It asks to be lived in our choices, our relationships, and our ways of moving through the world.

Living the catalyst means becoming aware of the triads at work within and around us, and learning to stand as the *"third presence"* wherever life seems divided. It means allowing tension to become a teacher instead of an enemy, letting the spark of creation rise from opposites we once thought irreconcilable.

This part of the journey turns from the universal to the intimate. It is no longer about patterns *"out there,"* but about how the catalyst moves through our speech, our silence, our conflicts, and our creativity. It is about living not as observers of the triad, but as participants in its dance.

Chapter 10

Working with the Law of Three

The Law of Three is not a distant abstraction; it is a living rhythm woven into every moment. Each choice we make, each conversation we enter, each challenge we face, all shaped by triadic movements, thesis, antithesis, and synthesis; push, pull, and release; shadow, light, and the meeting ground between them.

To work with the Law of Three is to notice where these forces are at play and to recognize the hidden catalyst that can transform them. It does not mean controlling outcomes or forcing harmony, but becoming attuned to the dance of tension and resolution as it unfolds.

Sometimes this means holding space for opposites without rushing to a conclusion. Other times, it means stepping in as the *"third presence"* that allows dialogue where there was only conflict, or vision where there was only confusion. In this way, the Law of Three becomes not just a lens for understanding but a compass for navigating life's complexity.

Working with it is less about technique and more about awareness; about seeing patterns that were always there and allowing them to guide us toward balance, creativity, and renewal.

Practical Ways to Identify Triads in Your Life

The Law of Three is not hidden; it is always at work. The challenge is noticing it. Triads often appear where tension, balance, and transformation meet. They can be subtle, quiet, or unmistakably dramatic. Here are ways to observe them:

1. Moments of Conflict:

When two opposing feelings, thoughts, or forces arise, pause and see if a third element naturally emerges. This could be a new idea, a compromise, or a fresh perspective that neither of the original forces anticipated.

2. Decision Points:

Choices rarely exist in perfect binaries. Notice where a third option arises, something that transforms the *"either/or"* into a new possibility. Somctimes it appears as intuition, sometimes as a solution that blends aspects of both extremes.

3. Patterns in Relationships:

Watch how dynamics shift when a third presence enters; it can be a mediator, an

observer, or even silence itself. This third factor often reshapes tension, turning a standoff into dialogue or misunderstanding into connection.

4. Cycles in Work or Creativity:

Look for recurring triads: problem, effort, resolution; inspiration, labor, outcome; planning, action, reflection. Triads often mark the rhythm of growth and innovation.

5. Nature and Surroundings:

Even in the environment, triads abound: Day, night, and twilight. Seed, growth, harvest. Predator, prey, ecosystem. Observing these patterns can reveal the hidden structure behind ordinary events.

The key is awareness. Triads often reveal themselves not as rules to follow, but as patterns to notice. They invite reflection, not prescription. They exist to be recognized, not forced, quietly guiding the flow of tension into transformation.

A young woman named Ada inherited a small plot of land in her village. She wanted to plant some food for her family, but also dreamed of creating a space where neighbors could gather, and children could play. Two visions pulled at her: Practicality versus beauty.

For weeks, she argued silently with herself. If she focused on crops, her family would be fed, but the land would look bare. If she built a garden for leisure, the soil would produce less, and hunger might strike.

Then, one morning, she noticed a patch of wildflowers growing along the edge of the land. They thrived effortlessly, attracting bees that helped pollinate her vegetable garden. At that moment, a third presence appeared: a solution neither of her original visions had foreseen. By integrating crops, flowers, and communal space, Ada turned tension into harmony.

The garden became more than survival or decoration; it became a living, balanced space, a triad made visible in soil, plant, and purpose.

This simple story shows how the Law of Three often operates quietly: Opposites create tension, and a third element emerges, sometimes from observation, sometimes from patience, but the end result is same: Transformation.

In Ada's garden, we see on a small scale what the universe enacts on a grand one. Just as her tension between survival and beauty gave rise to a creative third way, so too do stars form through the tension of gravity and heat, or societies find balance between tradition and progress.

The Law of Three does not only govern the cosmic or the abstract; it hums quietly within daily choices, guiding conflict toward resolution, opposites toward harmony, and ideas toward transformation.

Using the Principle to Make Decisions and Solve Problems

Decisions often appear as crossroads: Left or right, yes or no, stay or go. When life is viewed only in binaries, choices can feel heavy and limited. But the Law of Three reminds us that a third movement always exists: An insight, a bridge, or a synthesis that reshapes the tension.

1. From Opposition to Creation:

When two forces seem irreconcilable, ask: *"What could emerge if both were honored in some way?"* The third path is rarely a simple compromise; it is a transformation, something new that could not exist without the push and pull of the first two.

2. Inviting Time as the Third Element:

Sometimes the third force is not another option but time itself. In waiting, clarity forms. In patience, insight ripens. Problems that feel unsolvable in the moment often shift when time enters the equation.

3. The Role of Perspective:

When conflicts arise, imagine stepping outside of yourself to view the situation as an observer. This shift in perspective can act as the third element, bringing balance to the emotions and logic already in play.

4. Small Examples, Big Lessons:

- . **At work**: Faced with choosing between two competing strategies, the third way might be testing both on a small scale first, allowing evidence to guide the final decision.
- **In relationships**: When an argument pits one view against another, the third element may arrive as empathy, a willingness to see the
- other's need behind their words.

- **In personal dilemmas**: When torn between head and heart, the third way may appear as intuition, the quiet whisper that reconciles the two

The Law of Three does not erase difficulty; it reshapes it. Problems and decisions become less about choosing sides and more about allowing something new to be born.

The Art of Holding Tension Until Synthesis Emerges

Most of us are taught to escape tension as quickly as possible. We rush to decisions, patch conflicts with quick compromises, or silence opposing forces so that one may dominate. Yet, the Law of Three suggests that tension is not the enemy; it is the crucible.

When two opposing energies collide, they create pressure. Left unresolved, this pressure feels uncomfortable. But if one can hold the tension without collapsing into fear or rushing to an answer, a third force begins to stir. This is the essence of creation, the seedbed of transformation.

Nature models this for us. Consider the caterpillar inside its cocoon: Its form dissolves into chaos before wings appear. Or the atom, whose electrons spin in charged balance, holding the tension that allows matter to exist.

The cosmos itself thrives on tension, and so do we.

In personal life, the art of holding tension may look like:

- Sitting with a decision until its deeper meaning surfaces.
- Allowing silence in a difficult conversation until true understanding rises.
- Bearing the weight of inner conflict without rushing to suppress it, trusting that insight will eventually emerge.

To live the Law of Three is to cultivate the courage to wait inside the unknown. The synthesis comes not by force, but by faith in the unseen third presence that tension is preparing to reveal.

The Law of Three is not a formula to be applied, but a rhythm to be recognized. It reminds us that life is not built on binaries alone; that between yes and no, order and chaos, light and shadow, something new can be born, a Third, one that can act as the balance.

To see triads at work in our own lives is to discover that every conflict carries within it the possibility of transformation. Every decision, when held with patience, may open into a wider horizon. The art is not to force an answer, but to stay with the tension long enough for a deeper harmony to reveal itself.

In this way, the triads of the cosmos become the triads within us, guiding our choices, shaping our relationships, and reminding us that balance is never static but always alive, always evolving.

Chapter 11

The Power of Conscious Triads

Up to this point, we have seen how the Law of Three reveals itself in nature, the cosmos, the psyche, and the hidden fabric of human relationships. But there is a deeper shift that occurs when we move from simply noticing these patterns to working with them deliberately. This is the step from unconscious participation to conscious creation.

Most people live caught in dualities, pushed and pulled by opposites, reacting, rather than shaping. Yet, when we recognize the presence of a third force, we are no longer trapped in the struggle between two poles. We can stand at the center, perceiving not just the clash but the possibility it is concealing.

To live consciously with triads is to:

- Recognize when two opposing forces are shaping a situation.
- Resist the urge to collapse too quickly into one side or the other.

- Open space for the "*hidden third*" to emerge, bringing resolution, innovation, or transformation.

This awareness turns ordinary dilemmas into creative opportunities. It transforms conflict into dialogue, hesitation into patience, and chaos into the raw material for growth.

Conscious triads do not erase difficulty, but they change our relationship to it. Instead of being tossed about by the push and pull of life, we begin to work with its deeper rhythm. We become co-creators with the very pattern that shapes existence.

How Awareness Transforms Personal Growth

Awareness is the turning point. The moment we see that life is not a battle of opposites but a dance of three, something within us shifts. We stop identifying ourselves with just one force, desire or restraint, chaos or order, shadow or light, and begin to see how each belongs to a larger wholeness.

In personal growth, this awareness acts as a mirror. Instead of saying, *"I must destroy my impulses,"* we learn to listen to the id without being ruled by it. Instead of trying to be endlessly *"good,"* we allow the superego to guide without suffocating us. And instead of clinging to the ego as if it were the whole self, we recognize it as a negotiator, one voice among three.

Awareness transforms growth in three ways:

1. **Clarity**: We see that our struggles are not failures, but tensions waiting for a synthesis.

2. **Compassion**: We stop labeling parts of ourselves as *"bad"* and begin integrating them into balance.

3. **Creativity**: By holding opposites in awareness, we open ourselves to unexpected insights and possibilities.

In this way, growth ceases to be a rigid pursuit of perfection. It becomes a living dialogue between the forces within us, each voice respected, each tension honored, each resolution a doorway to a deeper self.

The Balance Between Action, Thought, and Being

Every human life is woven from three essential strands: action, thought, and being. They are the triad through which we shape our existence.

- Action propels us into the world. It is movement, choice, and the courage to bring ideas into form. Without it, dreams remain shadows.

- Thought gives action direction. It is reflection, analysis, and imagination. Without it, our movements scatter, lacking coherence.

- Being grounds both. It is presence, the silent awareness that exists before thought and beyond action. Without it, we become lost in endless doing or restless thinking.

Most of us tend to lean into one or two, neglecting the third. And because of this, we may become overactive, endlessly doing without reflection or stillness. Or we may overthink, turning in circles without acting. Or we may cling to being, retreating into stillness while the world calls for engagement.

Yet, when these three forces are balanced, something extraordinary emerges. Action becomes purposeful, thought becomes clear, and being becomes radiant.

The triad of action, thought, and being is not a hierarchy where one must dominate the others. It is a living rhythm, like breath: Inhale (being), pause (thought), exhale (action). To live in balance is to breathe life fully, without holding on too tightly to any single phase.

Personal growth deepens when we recognize this rhythm in ourselves, when we stop fighting against the imbalance and instead allow awareness to bring us back into harmony.

Long ago, three travelers set out to climb a mountain.

The first, Man of Action, rushed ahead, climbing fast and with great energy. But soon he grew exhausted, for he had not studied the path nor prepared his strength.

The second, Man of Thought, stayed behind, studying his maps. He traced every possible route in the dust, calculating risks. But he never took a step, and the mountain remained distant.

The third, Man of Being, sat quietly at the base, watching the clouds drift and the sun move across the sky. He felt peace in the stillness, but the mountain remained only a vision on the horizon.

At last, they met at the halfway point, tired, uncertain, and unsatisfied. They realized none of them could reach the summit alone. Thus, they chose to continue together.

The Man of Thought guided the way with his wisdom of the terrain. The Man of Action carried them forward with courage and strength. The Man of Being reminded them to rest, breathe, and see the beauty around them.

By the time they reached the summit, none claimed the victory as his own. The mountain had been climbed not by one, but by the triad of three: Action, thought, and being, all in balance.

Moving from Reaction to Creation

One of the greatest shifts in personal growth is moving from reaction to creation.

When we live in reaction, we are pulled by external forces, by other people's words, unexpected events, old habits, and unconscious fears. In this mode, the triad of action, thought, and being collapses into survival: Quick responses, scattered thinking, restless emotions. Reaction narrows us, keeping us bound to the past or defensive in the present.

Creation, however, arises when we consciously engage the triad.

- From being, we find presence; the pause before the storm of reaction.

- From thought, we choose direction; the clarity to see options rather than only triggers.

- From action, we move forward with intention, shaping new outcomes instead of repeating old patterns.

This shift does not mean denying reaction; it means transforming it into response, and then into creation. A harsh word can become the seed of deeper understanding. A setback can birth innovation. An inner conflict can awaken a new synthesis.

To live as a creator is not to control every outcome, but to walk in awareness that every moment holds the possibility of shaping something new. Let's look at this through an example:

Ify sat at the conference table, her jaw tight. Her colleague had just dismissed her idea with a careless wave of the hand, saying, *"That won't work."*

Her first impulse was to react, her mind flooded with sharp replies, her body tense with frustration. The Man of Action within her wanted to fight back immediately. The Man of Thought wanted to replay the insult over and over, building a case against

him. The Man of Being whispered faintly, but at first, she couldn't hear it.

Then she paused. Took a breath. In that pause, she remembered: she had a choice.

Instead of snapping back, she said calmly, "Maybe we're looking at the problem from different angles. Could we explore how both approaches might connect?"

The tone in the room shifted. Her colleague softened, the team leaned in, and what began as a dismissal turned into a breakthrough.

Later, Ify reflected. Her power had come not from suppressing her reaction, but from transforming it into creation. The triad within her, being, thought, and action, had aligned, and the outcome was something new.

Conscious triads transform how we move through life. When action, thought, and being are held in balance, we no longer react impulsively to tension but allow the space for something new to emerge. The pressures of conflict, uncertainty, and choice become fertile ground for insight, creativity, and growth.

Awareness of the triad invites us to see that every moment is a triadic field: two opposing forces and the hidden third that mediates and transforms. The journey from reaction to creation is not about eliminating tension, controlling outcomes, or mastering life in a rigid sense; it is about attuning ourselves to the rhythm of three and allowing the unseen catalyst to guide our movement.

In this way, personal growth, relationships, and even our work in the world become expressions of a deeper harmony. The Law of Three is no longer only a principle to observe; it becomes a living, dynamic force within us, shaping our choices, our presence, and the life we create.

Chapter 12

The Endless Spiral

Life does not move in straight lines. Decisions, growth, and creation are rarely linear; they unfold in spirals, circling back upon themselves, each loop higher, deeper, and more integrated than the last. The Law of Three is not a static pattern; it is a dynamic spiral, a living rhythm of tension, synthesis, and emergence.

Every triad in our lives, whether within our minds, relationships, or communities, carries the potential to expand. What begins as a simple recognition of opposing forces and a hidden third evolves over time, returning again and again, each time revealing deeper layers.

- The first encounter with a challenge may teach awareness.
- The second may inspire insight.
- The third may catalyze transformation.

This endless spiral mirrors nature itself: Seasons cycle, ecosystems renew, planets orbit. It mirrors the human psyche:

We revisit conflicts, emotions, and desires, each time with slightly more clarity and mastery. It mirrors society: Cultures rise, fall, and regenerate through tensions that are never fully resolved, but are always refined into a higher order.

The spiral reminds us that growth is iterative, continuous, and expansive. The Law of Three does not produce finality; it creates movement, evolution, and the unfolding of deeper wholeness.

The endless spiral is an invitation to participate consciously, to recognize recurring

patterns, and to allow each cycle to elevate us toward greater insight, creativity, and integration.

Long before humans walked the Earth, the universe was alive with tension. Clouds of gas and dust drifted silently in the void, pulled this way and that by gravity, pressure, and the unseen forces of energy. On their own, these clouds were chaotic, unstable, and seemingly inert.

Then, in the silent meeting of opposites, collapse and expansion, heat and cold, motion and stillness, a third force emerged. Nuclear fusion ignited within the densest clouds, sparking stars into being. These stars did not remain fixed; they moved, interacted, and lived out cycles of birth, life, and death, each one influencing the formation of galaxies, planets, and eventually, life itself.

The Law of Three was at play: tension created possibility, the unseen third catalyzed creation, and the spiral of evolution carried the universe onward. Every supernova seeded new matter, every orbit shaped new systems. The cosmos did not advance in a straight line; it spiraled, revisiting patterns, refining structures, and weaving an ever more intricate tapestry of existence.

Even now, as we look to the night sky, we witness the endless spiral: A universe in motion, where triads of force, matter, and energy continuously create, destroy, and transform. The cosmic dance is a living reminder that growth, whether in life or in the universe, is never final; it is iterative, cyclical, and infinitely expansive.

The cosmic spiral is more than a spectacle of stars; it is a mirror of our own lives. Just as galaxies form, collapse, and are reborn through cycles of tension and synthesis, we too experience recurring challenges, conflicts, and transformations.

- Moments of struggle may feel like collapse, but within the tension lies the hidden third, waiting to catalyze insight, resolution, or creativity.

- Decisions we make, once revisited over time, often reveal deeper layers of meaning, just as orbits refine the shape of a galaxy.

- Our relationships, careers, and inner growth unfold in spirals, returning us to lessons we thought were resolved, each time with new clarity and integration.

The endless spiral teaches that progress is iterative, not linear. Growth does not demand perfection; it asks for awareness, patience, and willingness to return to the triad again and again. Each cycle carries the potential for deeper harmony, just as the cosmos continuously evolves, balancing tension, synthesis, and emergence on an infinite scale.

In recognizing the spiral within ourselves, we begin to live not as victims of circumstance, but as participants in a cosmic rhythm, a rhythm where the Law of Three pulses through every choice, every challenge, and every transformation.

Why the Law of Three is Cyclical, Not Linear

The Law of Three does not operate like a straight arrow, moving from point A to point B. Life, growth, and creation are rarely linear; they unfold in cycles, spirals, and recurring patterns.

Every triad, be it thesis, antithesis, or synthesis, leads naturally to the next triad. The outcome of one cycle becomes the tension for the next. For example:

- A personal conflict may be resolved through insight, but new challenges arise, creating tension that calls for a deeper synthesis.
- A creative project may move from inspiration to struggle to completion, only to spark new ideas and innovations in its wake.
- In nature, seasons cycle, rivers flow, and ecosystems regenerate, demonstrating that equilibrium is dynamic, not static.

Cyclicity allows reflection, integration, and refinement. If triads were linear, growth would be a single leap from ignorance to mastery. But life works in spirals: We return to similar tensions, each time with more understanding, awareness, and capacity to act.

The spiral is also forgiving. It reminds us that missteps, mistakes, or unresolved tensions are not failures; they are necessary loops, essential to learning and transformation. The Law of Three thrives in this cyclical rhythm, revealing that progress is measured not in straight lines but in evolving, deepening cycles of creation.

Returning to the Beginning with Deeper Understanding

In the endless spiral of the Law of Three, beginnings are never truly lost; they return, transformed. Each cycle revisits familiar challenges, conflicts, or choices, but we approach them with new awareness, insight, and skill.

- A question once troubling may resurface, but we now perceive a hidden third that was invisible before.
- A recurring tension in a relationship may feel familiar, yet this time we respond with balance rather than reaction.
- A personal habit, challenge, or fear may reappear, inviting us to refine our approach, integrate lessons, and move closer to mastery.

The spiral reminds us that growth is iterative. Returning to the *"beginning"* is not regression; it is deepening.

Each loop carries the potential for synthesis, bringing together action, thought, and being, or shadow, light, and integration, in ways we could not have imagined the first time.

Life, like the cosmos, does not rush linearly toward perfection. It circles, revisits, and returns. And in each return, the hidden third, the catalyst, emerges again, guiding us toward greater wholeness, creativity, and understanding.

The endless spiral is a reminder: beginnings and endings are illusions. What truly matters is the rhythm of the triad and our conscious participation in its unfolding.

Closing Reflections

The Catalyst of Existence

The Law of Three is more than a principle; it is the catalyst of existence itself. Across the cosmos, in the cycles of nature, in the rhythms of human life, and in the depths of our own minds, triads pulse with creative potential. They are the hidden architecture of reality, shaping tension, synthesis, and emergence at every scale.

We have seen the triad in stars and galaxies, in ecosystems and seasons, in the dance of thought, action, and being, and in the delicate balance of relationships and societies. The third presence, the unseen catalyst, turns dualities into creation, challenges into insight, and conflict into growth.

To live with awareness of the Law of Three is to participate consciously in this ongoing dance. It invites patience in tension, openness to synthesis, and courage in transformation. It teaches that life is never a straight line but a spiral, returning to beginnings, revisiting lessons, and deepening understanding with each cycle.

Ultimately, the Law of Three reminds us that creation is continuous, balance is dynamic, and growth is never-ending.

By observing, feeling, and honoring the triads in our lives, we awaken to a reality where tension becomes opportunity, opposites become partners, and existence itself flows as a living, conscious catalyst.

In this way, we come to see that the world, and we ourselves, are not passive observers but active participants in the eternal unfolding of the triad, the hidden pattern, the catalyst, and the endless spiral of life.

Conclusion

Embracing the Catalyst

Throughout this journey, we have traced the Law of Three from the vastness of the cosmos to the intricacies of the human mind, from societal structures to the rhythms of personal growth. We have seen that triads, opposites bridged by a hidden third, are not abstract ideas but living patterns that shape everything: stars, ecosystems, societies, relationships, and the very essence of self.

The Law of Three is the catalyst of existence. It transforms tension into insight, conflict into creation, and cycles of challenge into spirals of growth. It reminds us that life is never linear, but dynamic, iterative, and ever-unfolding. Each triad, each cycle, each unseen force is an invitation to participate consciously in the ongoing dance of creation.

By observing and honoring these triads:

- We learn to hold tension without fear, allowing insight and synthesis to emerge.

- We balance action, thought, and being, moving from reaction into creation.

- We recognize patterns in ourselves, our relationships, and the world, awakening to a deeper harmony that mirrors the rhythms of the universe.

The journey of understanding the Law of Three is also a journey into ourselves. Every conflict, every choice, every cycle carries within it the potential for growth, for creativity, and for transformation. To embrace this law is to embrace life in its fullest complexity and to participate consciously in the eternal spiral of becoming.

And so, as the chapters close, the story does not end. Like the endless spiral itself, awareness of the Law of Three carries forward into each decision, each relationship, each moment, beckoning us to notice, to balance, and to allow the hidden third to guide us toward ever-deepening wholeness.

Life, in its infinite complexity, is a triad in motion. And we, when conscious, are both witnesses and catalysts.

www.ingramcontent.com/pod-product-compliance
Lightning Source LLC
La Vergne TN
LVHW051044210926
848486LV00001B/15
* 9 7 9 8 2 9 5 4 8 2 8 7 8 *